NATIVE AMERICAN HISTORY *for* Kids

NATIVE AMERICAN
HISTORY *for* Kids

WITH 21 ACTIVITIES

KAREN BUSH GIBSON

CHICAGO
REVIEW
PRESS

Library of Congress Cataloging-in-Publication Data

Gibson, Karen Bush.

    Native American history for kids : with 21 activities / Karen Bush Gibson.

        p. cm.

    Includes bibliographical references.

    ISBN 978-1-56976-280-6 (pbk.)

    1. Indians of North America—History—Juvenile literature.   2. Indians of North America—Social life and customs—Juvenile literature.   3. Indians of North America—History—Study and teaching (Elementary)   4. Indians of North America—History—Study and teaching (Elementary)—Activity programs.   5. Creative activities and seat work—Juvenile literature.   I. Title.

E77.4.G53 2010

970.004'97—dc22

2010005695

Cover design: Monica Baziuk

Cover images: (Front) Totem pole, pottery, Mesa Verde: Shutterstock Images. Tribal leaders on horseback, Alaskan Native family, Chief Joseph, Lakota tipi camp: Library of Congress. (Back) Alaskan Native family, buffalo hunting party: Library of Congress. Carved bear fetish: Shutterstock Images.

Interior design: Monica Baziuk

Interior photos on pages 2, 3, 21 (Mission Concepcion), 63, and 67 courtesy of the author. All other photos courtesy of the Library of Congress unless otherwise noted.

Interior maps: Chris Erichsen

Interior illustrations: Laura D'Argo

Published by Chicago Review Press, Incorporated

814 North Franklin Street

Chicago, Illinois 60610

ISBN 978-1-56976-280-6

Printed in the United States of America

TO MY CHOCTAW FAMILY

CONTENTS

NATIVE AMERICAN HISTORY TIME LINE

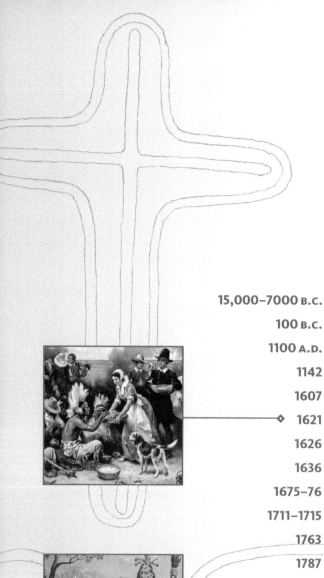

15,000–7000 B.C.	Paleo-Indian era
100 B.C.	First mound cultures begin
1100 A.D.	Cliff cities built in Southwest by Ancestral Puebloans
1142	Iroquois Confederacy constitution written
1607	Chief Powhatan captures Captain John Smith
1621	The Pilgrims at Plymouth and the Wampanoag sign a peace treaty
1626	Peter Minuit buys Manhattan Island from the Lenni Lenape
1636	The Pequot War occurs
1675–76	King Philip's War
1711–1715	Tuscarora Indian War
1763	Chief Pontiac leads the Ottawa in battle against the British
1787	First federal treaty is made with the Delaware Nation
1803	The Louisiana Purchase adds to the United States' territory
1804–06	Lewis and Clark chart the western territory with the help of Sacagawea, a Shoshone Indian
1808–12	Tecumseh and his brother, Tenskwatawa, found Prophetstown as a Native American confederacy
1815	The Seminole Wars begin
1821	The federal government begins moving Cherokee, Creek, Seminole, Choctaw, and Chickasaw west of the Mississippi River

1828	Sequoyah and Elias Boudinot begin publishing the *Cherokee Phoenix*
1830	Indian Removal Act is passed
1834	Congress creates Indian Territory
1835–42	Second Seminole War
1838	Cherokee are forcibly removed to Indian Territory
1849	The Bureau of Indian Affairs transfers from the War Department to the Department of the Interior
1860–64	The Navajo War breaks out in New Mexico Territory
1864	Sand Creek Massacre
1876	Lakota defeat George Armstrong Custer in the Battle of the Little Bighorn
1877	Nez Percé leader Chief Joseph surrenders
1879	Carlisle Indian boarding school is established
1890	Wounded Knee Massacre
1886	Geronimo surrenders
1887	The Dawes Act passes
1889	Wovoka leads to the beginning of the Ghost Dance religion
1924	Native Americans granted citizenship and voting rights
1934	Indian Reorganization Act is passed
1944	The National Congress of American Indians (NCAI) is formed
1968	Indian Civil Rights Act passes; American Indian Movement (AIM) is created
1969–71	Occupation of Alcatraz Island
1973	Occupation at Wounded Knee on the Pine Ridge Reservation
1978	Indian Child Welfare Act and American Indian Religious Freedom Act pass
1988	Indian Gaming Regulatory Act allows tribes to conduct gaming
1990	Native American Languages Act and Native American Grave Protection and Repatriation Act are passed by Congress
1996	President Clinton authorizes November as National American Indian Month
2001	John Herrington becomes the first Native American in space

NOTE TO READERS

M ANY OF the geographic names used in this book are not those used at the time that early cultures lived there. However, they've been used throughout the book so that you can get a better sense of where tribes lived and where events took place.

PREFACE

A COMPREHENSIVE BOOK on Native American history is an impossible task. There are 562 federally recognized nations or tribes, which means there are a minimum of 562 histories. The actual number of groups is higher because many nations include different subgroups or bands, some nations with dwindling populations joined other nations with more resources, and not all Native American tribes are recognized by the federal government.

Native Americans aren't all alike any more than all Americans are alike. To say that all Hopi, Seminole, and Lakota people are alike because they are part of a larger Native American group is the same as saying that all British, Spanish, and Greek people are alike because they are from Europe.

Native American nations have different languages, customs, and histories. It would be a disservice to generalize, so whenever possible, efforts should be made to identify the specific nation. Sometimes that's not possible, and "Native American" is used. Other people prefer "American Indian." "First Nation" is used in Canada, and "First American" is another possibility.

White men originally wrote American history because they were the ones in power. Unfortunately, they also wrote that history with cultural bias. For thousands of years, Native American history was an oral history passed down from generation to generation. This system worked until altercations with European Americans destroyed many traditions.

Even when the white culture wanted to accurately record Native American history, there wasn't any guarantee that the entire truth, or even a story that approached the truth, was being told. Some stories belong to the tribe or nation. They are sacred, and to share them outside of the group was against beliefs. According to author Lucy Tapahonso, "To Navajos, a person's worth is determined by the stories and songs she or he knows, because it is by this knowledge that an individual is directly linked to the history of the entire group." Additionally, after centuries of abuse and broken promises, many Native Americans hesitated to share their stories with the Euro-American culture.

Since the latter half of the 20th century, more social scientists and historians have tried to correct the inaccurate histories by studying the ethnohistory of Native Americans. Ethnohistory uses both historical and ethnographic information—including music, oral traditions, art, language, and customs—to gain more understanding about a culture.

Still, incorrect information continues to exist in books, television, movies, and society. Everyone has a responsibility to verify and correct information when possible.

In this book, every effort has been made to relate factual information. We owe this to Native Americans of all nations. Sharing a correct and rich history benefits us all. As Pearl Buck said, "If you want to understand today, you have to search yesterday."

NATIVE AMERICAN
HISTORY *for* Kids

THE FIRST PEOPLE

THE SOUND of a hawk shattered the silence as rancher Richard Wetherill and his brother-in-law climbed to the top of the mesa. From the top of the flat-topped hill, they hoped to see where several cattle had wandered. But the Native American guides who had accompanied them refused to go farther—they shook their heads and communicated something about the "Ancient Ones."

The snow on that December day in 1888 made it difficult to see, which may have caused Wetherill to rub his eyes at what he saw next—there was a city perched in an opening between the cliffs. Large sandstone buildings with almost 100 windows and doors sat silently in the falling snow. The same sandstone lined a number of circular shapes in the ground. The city of stone showed no signs of life. It had been deserted for over 500 years.

Mesa Verde

THE PLACE that Wetherill stumbled upon was called Mesa Verde, Spanish for "green table," located in the southwestern corner of Colorado. It is one of many ancient abandoned communities in the Southwest, particularly in New Mexico, Colorado, Utah, and Arizona. From 550 to 1300 A.D., thousands of people lived and worked in this area. They carved and constructed multistory buildings from sandstone while people in other parts of the world still lived in caves or primitive huts.

One of the main activities of this civilization was making sure there was enough food to survive. A young girl of the time would probably help her family farm corn, beans, and squash.

Cliff Palace at Mesa Verde National Park.

After planting the crops with digging sticks and irrigating them with nearby water, the people waited until harvest time. They spent their free time socializing and playing games.

At harvest, the girl might carry ears of corn in a basket woven from yucca or other plant fibers. She would take the basket to her home, located in a building shared with fifteen other families of her clan. The girl would climb two ladders to reach her third-floor home. In a small room, her mother would sit on her knees, grinding corn for the family's meals. A black-and-white clay pot would sit on the fire cooking a dinner of stew. The smoke from the fire rose up the center of the room until it exited out the hole in the ceiling.

The cliff dwellings faced south, so they enjoyed the warmth of the sun in the winter. Small stones called chinking stones filled the gaps between the sandstone blocks that the buildings were made from. Mortar from soil, ash, and water cemented the parts of the walls together. The thickness of the walls kept out the worst of the summer heat, too.

In addition to the cliff dwellings where families lived, Mesa Verde contained below-ground circular chambers, known as kivas. Kivas probably served as meeting places for special gatherings. Clan leaders might meet in kivas to settle disputes, hold council meetings, or conduct religious ceremonies. The largest kiva at

CHACO CANYON

Mesa Verde is just one of many settlements left by ancient people. Another is in Chaco Canyon, located in New Mexico's Navajo (also known as Diné) country. Mesa Verde was made a national park in 1906. Chaco Canyon was part of the first group of sites President Theodore Roosevelt gave national monument status in 1907. White Americans first heard of the spectacular ruins in 1849 when the U.S. military recorded their existence and did some excavating. Archaeologists were able to date the buildings in Chaco Canyon because of the large amount of ponderosa pines used in the construction. Tree ring data proves that building began in the ninth century.

Chaco Canyon has been the source of much curiosity and study. It's estimated that at least 5,000 people lived at Chaco Canyon around 1100 A.D. Although it was a primitive time period, these people were able to build a city and a key center of trade with roads leading in and out.

The people who lived in Chaco Canyon didn't construct cliff dwellings, they made large stone buildings called "great houses."

Pueblo Bonito ruins at Chaco Culture National Historic Park.

The largest was the five-level Pueblo Bonito, which contained hundreds of rooms. Both the great houses and the cliff dwellings resemble apartment buildings with many floors and rooms. The homes of the Ancestral Puebloans predated apartment buildings by over 600 years—the first apartment building in the United States wasn't built until 1882, in New York. The degree of technical skill needed to create such communities continues to astound visitors.

Cliff Palace, 12 feet deep and 50 feet across, was located in the center of the village.

The Navajo, who live primarily in New Mexico and Arizona, first named the people of these ancient abandoned villages "Anasazi," which means "evil ones" or "ancient enemies." Anasazi was also the name that white people first used when they began exploring the different ruins, trying to solve the mystery of what happened to the people who disappeared so suddenly, leaving baskets, pottery, and tools behind. The correct name for these people who lived over 800 years ago is Ancestral Puebloans.

While the Ancestral Puebloan girl helped with the farming and her mother ground corn, her brother and father would hunt in nearby forests with spears or bows and arrows. The deer and rabbit provided meat to eat and skins to keep people warm in the winter. When food from farming and hunting was scarce, the people searched for food among the wild plants. Much of each day was spent gathering or preparing food.

Late in the 20th century, scientists determined that the people didn't disappear, they just migrated. The current preferred theory states that an extended drought forced the inhabitants to move to locations where they could grow crops. Although the Ancestral Puebloans had experienced dry periods before, a 25-year drought at the end of the 1200s made farming almost impossible. Additionally, the people had been living in the same area for over 700 years, so other resources such as firewood had likely been depleted.

The descendants of the people who lived in the great houses and cliff dwellings live today as members of the Hopi, Zuni, and dozens of other nations known as Pueblo nations. Like their ancestors, many Pueblo communities depend on agriculture.

Cliff Palace kivas.

Mississippian Cultures

OVER 1,000 miles east of the cliff dwellings, other groups of people lived a different kind of life. They, too, had cities, which they built on mounds of earth. Flat-topped hills, reaching up to 35 feet high and spreading across many acres, supported buildings made from wood and mud. Buildings on the largest mounds most likely served as temples or official residences for leaders. Buildings on smaller mounds served other purposes, such as places for burial. However, when a leader died, his home was often burned or torn down, and the leader buried in its place. Archaeologists estimate that hundreds, perhaps thousands, of workers carried baskets, each filled with 60 pounds of soil, to add to the mound. This process of building, tearing down, burying, and adding soil to the mound might be repeated many times, causing the mounds to grow larger over time. In earlier periods, prosperous people were laid to rest in cone-shaped or round mounds. Mound civilizations were discovered in the Mississippi and Ohio river valleys. Scientists refer to the civilizations that flourished there between 100 and 1700 A.D. as the Mississippian cultures. More informally, native people of this era are called mound builders.

A city might include several mounds around a plaza. A village of mud-and-thatch houses and farms sat on the outer edges of the mounds. Like the Ancestral Puebloans, the Mississippians grew corn, beans, and squash. Nearby rivers provided irrigation for crops and a way to travel to other cities to trade or to attend festivals. Both copper from the Great Lakes and conch shells from the Gulf of Mexico found their way to Mississippian communities in the Mississippi and Ohio valleys.

Religious ceremonies were an important aspect of Mississippian cultures and provided

Mound builders gathering crops.

religious leaders with the power to govern all aspects of a community. As the cultures grew, they became more warlike. Weapons have been discovered almost exclusively in newer mounds. As their land became overused and no longer productive for farming, these people also moved on.

WHERE OUR PEOPLE CAME FROM— THE SACRED MOUND, NANIH WAIYA

One of the mound building cultures were the Choctaw people. According to a Choctaw historian named Horatio Cushman, the Choctaw people were in Mississippi when mammoths became extinct. Therefore, by the time Choctaws first encountered Spanish explorer Hernando de Soto in 1540, the Choctaw had a thriving agricultural culture in place.

Northeast of Philadelphia, Mississippi, a large rectangular mound stands 25 feet high. The 218-foot-long, 140-foot-wide mound is called Nanih Waiya, which is Choctaw for "Leaning Hill." Some scholars believe the spelling is actually "Nanih Waya," which would change the meaning to "Fruitful Hill" or "Productive Hill." Nearby pottery shards indicate the mound was created around 100 A.D., but according to Cushman's account of Choctaw history, the sacred hill would likely be much older.

According to Choctaw legend, the mound gave birth to the Choctaw people by bringing them from the underworld to populate the land above—the Choctaw emerged from a nearby cave. Since the beginning of documented Choctaw history and culture, the hill has been considered holy. Today, the State of Mississippi protects it as a state park. When two-thirds of the Choctaw people were forcibly moved to Oklahoma in the 19th century, they named their first capitol Nanih Waiya in honor of this sacred mound.

By Land or by Sea

So how did Native Americans first arrive on the North American continent? A popular theory accepted for many years was that some people migrated through Asia and crossed a strip of land between Siberia and Alaska approximately 13,000 years ago. A body of water known as the Bering Strait separates Siberia from Alaska by 55 miles. But during the most recent ice age, the Pleistocene Ice Age, it's believed that the large number of glaciers that formed from water freezing on land caused sea levels to drop about 300 feet, creating a land bridge between Asia and North America that made travel between them possible. Two huge ice sheets covered Canada and the northern United States during this time period known as the Ice Age. However, scientists have found evidence that shows an ice-free corridor existed between these two North American ice sheets that would have allowed people to migrate south from Alaska into the United States, leading to the Clovis culture, thought to represent the first Native Americans on the continent, approximately 11,500 years ago.

Less than 50 years after Wetherill stumbled on the ancient ruins known as Mesa Verde, a 22-year-old man named Ridgely Whiteman was trying to get someone to believe that there were mammoth bones in the basins south of Clovis, New Mexico. University of Pennsylvania graduate student Edgar B. Howard arrived in 1932 and agreed that the area was definitely worth investigating. After contacting paleontologists and arranging for crews, Howard and company began digging the following year.

At first, the teams found artifacts similar to those uncovered about 200 miles north at Wild Horse Gulch near Folsom, New Mexico, an area that had already been excavated. The Folsom site revealed bison bones with embedded spear points, and the Clovis site looked like another hunting camp from the same era.

The teams continued digging, uncovering scraping tools and chopping tools. But when they found a mammoth bone embedded with a four-inch spearhead, they knew they had found a second, older culture, because mammoth were extinct in the age of the artifacts at the Folsom site. The Clovis site spear point differed from the two-inch spear points found at Folsom. Not only was the Clovis point twice as large, but its base contained a groove not found on the thinner Folsom spear point.

Howard and many other paleontologists and archaeologists were certain that the Clovis artifacts were from an earlier culture. Carbon dating, developed in the 1950s, later confirmed it. The dating of the Clovis site fit with land bridge theories.

Other points like the ones found in Clovis turned up at archeological sites, particularly in

Origins of People

MANY NATIVE cultures have legends or myths about the origin of their culture, often referred to as creation stories.

Alsea

In the beginning, many people gathered together. The Creator sent away two people—a husband and wife—to start their own tribe. The Creator sent away two more people to start another tribe, and another.

Iroquois

There was once a floating island with a beautiful, fragrant tree where people gathered. One day, the Great Ruler said that it was time to make a new place where other people could grow. He pulled the council tree from the ground to reveal a great cloud sea. The cloud sea summoned Ata-en-sic, who was with child. The animals of the cloud sea were alarmed at this new creature and didn't know what to do, but the Turtle agreed to carry her. She gave birth to twin sons, who were the spirits of good and evil. One brother created the sun and light; the other darkness. Then the brothers filled the new world with their creations. The good brother created beauty and things that helped the humans. The bad brother created things that destroyed his brother's work, such as tornados and floods.

Apache

In the beginning, Tepeu and Gucumatz sat and thought, and whatever they thought was created. They created the Earth, mountains, trees, sky, and animals. But Tepeu and Gucumatz wanted praise, so they tried to create beings out of clay. The first clay beings fell apart when they got wet. The wood beings didn't work either. With the help of Coyote, Crow, Mountain Lion, and Parrot, they created four new beings that became the ancestors of the Apache.

Research and read other Native American creation or origin stories, preferably one from the Native American culture that lives or lived in your area. Then try your hand at writing your own.

Chronology of a Lifetime

ANTHROPOLOGISTS AND other scientists spend a lot of time trying to figure out the timing of different activities that were part of specific Native American cultures. It's a very difficult task.

In this activity, have a person write out six events that occurred in his or her lifetime, with no clues as to the timing. The six events should be written on individual strips of paper. Here is an example:

My sister was born.
My family visited Mexico.
My grandfather died.
Our dog, Rascal, joined the family.
My best friend moved away.
I broke my leg at the playground.

Shuffle the pieces of paper. Try to place the six events in the proper order. If possible, do this activity with someone you don't know well.

the southeastern United States, but some sites showed differences. Not all the spear points were fluted or made with grooves like those found in New Mexico.

The nonfluted spear points belonged to a later Paleo-Indian group called the Plano culture. Like the Clovis and Folsom cultures, hunting was a way of life for the Plano people. Just as the mammoth became extinct after the Clovis period, so did the early bison from the Folsom period. The Plano groups hunted the modern bison, or "buffalo," on the Great Plains. In the East, deer and elk were probably the animal of choice.

COOPER SKULL

In 1994, archaeologists at the Cooper site in northwestern Oklahoma discovered a bison skull with a red zigzag painted on it. Located at a kill site, the skull was dated at more than 10,000 years old, making it the oldest painted object in North America. A kill site is a place where large animals were killed and butchered long ago.

Why the big fuss over a painted skull? Actually, the skull tells far more about a people than the fact that they hunted bison. It identified the use of hematite for painting in a hunting ritual, a fact not previously known of Paleo-Indian people. Painting the skull with a distinctive design meant something; it was tied to some aspect of belief the people had. Hunting wasn't just a matter of getting food—a ritual was taking place, probably led by a shaman or spiritual man. Some groups of native hunters, including the Cree and Assiniboine, placed offerings such as tobacco, scarlet cloth, and bison skulls at the base of poles in the middle of a corral. Hunters needed a way to trap bison in close proximity in order to kill them with spears, and these sacrificial offerings were believed to draw bison to an enclosed area. Perhaps the decorated Cooper Skull was placed at the location as a good luck charm for future hunts. Damage found on the Cooper Skull may have resulted from being trampled under the hooves of hundreds of thundering bison.

The Cooper Skull currently resides at the Sam Noble Museum of Natural History at the University of Oklahoma in Norman.

Monte Verde

ANTHROPOLOGISTS THOUGHT they had it all figured out. The people who became Native Americans crossed over from Asia, leading to the Paleo-Indian groups: Clovis, Folsom, and Plano. Afterward, the Archaic people, such as the Ancestral Puebloans and the Mound Builders of the East, built their civilizations.

But then, Monte Verde.

In the 1990s, scientists located an ancient camp along a creek bank in a wooded, hilly area in Chile. Years of study led to the conclusion that the dwellings, tools, and other artifacts were at least a thousand years *older* than those found at the Clovis site in New Mexico. The world's most prominent archaeologists traveled to South America and verified that a hunting and gathering society camped at Monte Verde at least 12,500 years ago, making it the oldest known native site on the American continents.

It's believed that approximately 20 to 30 people lived at Monte Verde for about a year. About 12 huts stood in the settlement, built from wood planks and covered in animal hides held down with tent stakes that were found at the dig. Some of the stakes and poles still had cords tied with overhand knots. The Monte Verde people were hunters, but they also were gatherers, collecting berries, chestnuts, mushrooms, potatoes, and marsh grasses during different seasons of the year. For variety, they also traveled to the Pacific Ocean, about 30 miles away, for shellfish.

The reason that archaeologists were able to learn so much about Monte Verde is that it was covered with a peat bog. Over time, oxygen in the air causes items to decay. Peat bogs effectively keep oxygen away, allowing items to be preserved. The peat bog at Monte Verde was so effective that it even preserved a child's footprint near a cooking pit.

Most interesting of all, however, was that the people of Monte Verde couldn't have crossed the Bering Strait—there wouldn't have been a land bridge or an ice-free corridor at the time they would have had to migrate. In other words, the people of Monte Verde didn't migrate from Asia through Alaska. Perhaps, at some point, the people of Monte Verde traveled by boat up the Pacific

CAVE PAINTINGS

Before the Ancestral Puebloans created their amazing structures, early people in North America lived in pit houses in the ground. Before that, they lived in caves. Many ancient people throughout the world have communicated by painting on cave walls. Early rock and cave paintings record information about hunts or battles. Perhaps the paintings even served some ceremonial purpose. One of the most famous Native American rock art sites is the Chumash Indian Painted Cave in Santa Barbara, California.

Pictographs

BEFORE WRITTEN languages, some Native American nations recorded history with pictographs, which are symbols or pictures that describe an event.

Plains tribes in particular often had calendars in which they recorded the most important event of a year. The Kiowa, a Plains tribe, documented events twice a year. In the late 19th century and early 20th century, Silver Horn was the calendar keeper. His pictorials of what occurred during the summer and winter seasons provide a glimpse into Kiowa history. Sometimes a pole was included in the summer pictures. This always meant that the Sun Dance had taken place. An owl in the picture often meant that someone had died.

Look at some common pictograph symbols and what they represent:

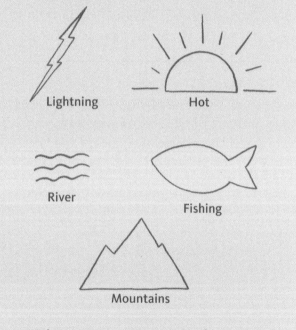

Lightning

Hot

River

Fishing

Mountains

Within your own nation or tribe (family, class, or group of friends), decide on the five most important events of the past month. Record these events with pictographs.

coast and settled in the United States. A coastal migration would have been faster, and the ocean would have provided food along the way.

This provides yet another theory as to where the first Americans came from. Knowledge about the ice age and Monte Verde suggests that if people didn't arrive during the period when the land bridge or the ice-free corridor was available, then people either arrived from a different place than previously thought, or people have lived in the Americas for at least 20,000 years. It could also indicate that early people in the Americas came from various geographical locations.

Language and DNA

SCIENCE LOOKS at facts to support or disprove theories. In searching for the earliest Native Americans, scientists such as archaeologists and anthropologists study ruins and objects left behind, such as pottery and cave paintings, to learn about the people who lived long ago.

Physical anthropologists who study human skeletons say that the similarities and differences in skulls tell a lot about where people came from. For example, many of the skulls found in North America that are more than 8,000 years old are long and narrow, which is more similar to the skulls of Europeans than those of modern Native Americans. However, a 9,200-year-old Nevada skeleton called the Wizard's Beach Man does reveal similarities to modern Native Americans. Native American critics believe that differences in skull shapes mean nothing because people from long ago looked different from people of today.

As knowledge and technology expand, we also look for answers from different places. One of these is linguistics, the study of languages. By studying language patterns and history, linguists look for connections between cultures in different parts of the country or from different periods in history.

Before Europeans arrived in the Americas, it's estimated that there were about 1,000 native languages. Linguists who specialize in Native American languages have found almost 200 language families, some with very complex grammar. The variety and differences among the languages suggest that the people that make up Native American groups came from many, many different places.

Early DNA research provided conflicting information about the relationship between early Native Americans and other populations. A study at the University of California at Davis, published in 2009, identified a gene common in most of the 41 Native American populations they tested. This marker, called the 9-repeat allele, was not present in any of the 54 Eurasian,

THE FIRST ARCHAEOLOGISTS

Thomas Jefferson.

An archaeologist is a scientist who studies humans and cultures of the past by recovering and examining evidence, such as pottery, tools, and even trash. Thomas Jefferson is often credited as the father of American archaeology because of his curiosity about Native Americans.

In the state of Virginia where Jefferson lived, mounds provided evidence of early Native American cultures. Additionally, Jefferson had discovered bones of ancient people near his Monticello home. He also had a mastodon tooth from a western Virginia site near the city of Saltville. Jefferson believed clues about the history of Native Americans could also be found in the languages they spoke. Due to his curiosity, Jefferson sent Meriwether Lewis and William Clark to learn more about the Native Americans of the West in hopes of answering his questions.

Archaeology and the closely related science anthropology have provided more information about ancient native people. In so doing, these sciences have also contributed to the destruction of cultures by removing items or communicating erroneous information, either intentionally or by accident. Some descendants of ancient cultures believe that these social scientists have contributed to discrimination through stereotyping cultural groups.

The first known anthropological study in America was documented in the 1851 paper, "League of the Ho-de-no-saunee, or Iroquois" by Lewis Henry Morgan, who received an enormous amount of help from a young Seneca man, Ely S. Parker. A century later, in 1952, Edward P. Dozier graduated from the University of California at Los Angeles with a doctorate in anthropology. As a member of the Pueblo band, Dozier was the nation's first Native American anthropologist. Throughout his career, Dozier had to balance his native values with scientific methods. His work led to the establishment of an American Indian Studies program at the University of Arizona. Today, the number of American Indian Studies programs at universities, and the number of Native American anthropologists, archaeologists, and ethnologists, continues to grow.

It's Tool Time

ARCHAEOLOGISTS USE the discovery of tools to identify and learn more about specific cultures. Tools serve many purposes in all cultures. Today you might use a hammer, but long ago people hammered with rocks. Today you use a needle and thread to sew, but people once created sewing needles out of bone and thread from the sinew of animals. From the earliest days, tools have been used for hunting, skinning, cutting, and cooking. People look at a need and create a tool to help them with that need.

Now it's time to build your own tool. Have you ever tried to reach for something that is too high? Sure, you can climb on top of a chair, but that means having to move it or worry about falling off the chair. What if you could make a tool to grab what you need?

Materials
◆ Rope, half the width of your tube but three times as long
◆ Pencil or knitting needle
◆ Long plastic tube, at least as long as your arm

Make a slipknot in the middle of the rope. First, create a loop in the middle of the rope. Wrap one end of the rope around the loop, and then create another loop that you pull through the first loop.

If tied correctly, one end of your rope will tighten the knot, and other will undo it. You might want to mark the end that will tighten it with a piece of tape or by tying another knot in the end of it.

Put a pencil or knitting needle through the loop and tighten the knot around it. This will help you pull the slipknot through the plastic tube without it coming undone.

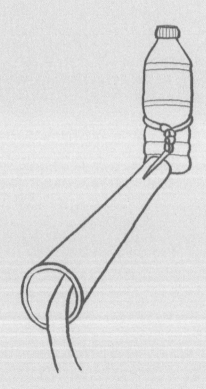

After you've pulled your knot through the tube, make the knot bigger again and remove the pencil or knitting needle. When you need to retrieve something (nonbreakable only), use the tube of your tool to place the loop of rope around the object. Then pull the knot tight with the correct end of your rope. This should secure your object while you bring it down.

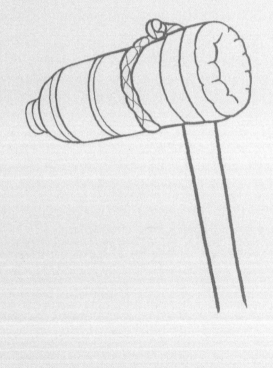

Oceanian, and African groups tested. From these results, scientists suggest that the earliest Native Americans must have been isolated from these other populations for thousands of years.

Some Native Americans question why scientists claim that their ancestors must have come across a land bridge or from somewhere else by boat. They asked, why couldn't Native Americans have always been present in North America? The varied information uncovered by archaeologists and anthropologists can't rule that out. Indeed, research suggests that a variety of migrations from different areas took place at different times. Yet it's not just the origins of Native Americans that are being sought, but the origins of human life.

Learning more about the origins of Native Americans is an ongoing project, requiring the joint efforts of archaeologists, linguists, and biologists. New discoveries are constantly being made. Some of them may replace today's theories.

2

IN SEARCH of the CITY of GOLD

WHEN **CHRISTOPHER** Columbus first landed in the Americas in 1492, he and his crew were greeted by the indigenous (native) people who lived on an island in the Bahamas. Columbus suggested that the natives could provide labor—slave labor—for the Spanish while learning European ways. Other European explorers followed Columbus, but most had similar ideas—to conquer the Native Americans.

Europeans continued to explore to the west and soon claimed Mexico for their own. When they reached the land that would eventually become the

United States, a few conquistadors traveled in the Southeast. Ponce de Leon sailed to Florida, and Hernando de Soto explored Mississippi. However, the majority of Spanish explorers journeyed from Mexico through the southwestern United States in search of gold.

The Southwest

MORE THAN 100 years before the Spanish arrived, the Southwest was already a busy place with people belonging to many Native American nations. Before 1400, Shoshonean-

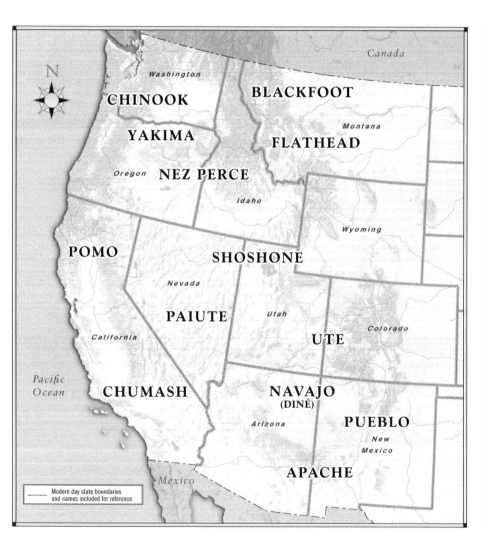

PONCE DE LEON AND THE FLORIDA NATIVES

After sailing with Columbus in 1493, Juan Ponce de Leon was given permission by Spain to search for Bimini, an island rumored to be home to the Fountain of Youth. According to legend, one drink from this fountain would keep a person from growing older.

Ponce de Leon.

In his search for the legendary fountain, Ponce de Leon landed on what he thought was an island. Unknown to the explorer, it was a peninsula. He named the location Florida because of its many flowers and claimed the land for Spain. Ponce de Leon first arrived on the east coast of Florida and founded what became Saint Augustine, today the oldest city in the United States.

Ponce de Leon undertook his last voyage in 1521 to colonize Florida's west coast. The native Calusa didn't want any settlements near their village. They greeted the Spanish with arrows. Ponce de Leon received an arrow to the thigh and died.

speaking tribes, such as the Ute and Paiute, hunted in the Colorado mountains and spent winters in northern New Mexico. Their neighbors were the generally peaceful Pueblo tribes who established villages and spent their days farming. Pueblos created terraced farms, using nearby deep gullies and reservoirs for water.

Many other nations in the region were hunters and gatherers—Comanche, Apache, Cheyenne, Kiowa, and the groups that Europeans came to call the Sioux. These nomadic groups rarely stayed in one place long, preferring to follow food sources, mainly bison. Occasionally, tribes battled one another over hunting rights in an area.

More Europeans arrived in 1536—Spanish explorers. Most were looking for the mythical city of gold called El Dorado. The legend of El Dorado promised that whoever found the city would receive great riches. One of the most active and well-known searchers was Francisco Vasquez de Coronado, who began extensive exploration in 1540. Unable to locate El Dorado in South America or Mexico, the Spanish began looking elsewhere.

EL DORADO: CITY OF GOLD

The legend of El Dorado (meaning "The Golden One") originated in South America, where the Muisca people made offerings by tossing gold into Colombia's Lake Guatavita in much the same way that people today toss a coin in a fountain and make a wish. When the Spanish explorers arrived and found gold around the lake, the legend began. The Spanish took away much of the gold and speculated that the New World must have other places of riches, perhaps even a city of gold.

(LEFT) Spanish conquistadors.
(RIGHT) Zuni pueblo.

A Franciscan priest, Friar Marcos de Niza, reported seeing a city of riches to the north of Mexico called Cibola. Marcos had actually been to the pueblo of the Zuni tribe located in New Mexico. According to the Zuni, Marcos had a guide named Estevan who demanded Zuni turquoise and women. The Zuni refused and killed him. Marcos fled back to Mexico in fear for his life. Once he returned home, he told outlandish stories of the Seven Cities of Cibola.

With 300 conquistadors and 1,000 Mexican natives, Coronado headed north into New Mexico to discover these cities of riches. Instead, he stumbled upon a small, crowded Zuni pueblo. The Zuni found the animals that accompanied Coronado quite interesting. The Spanish soldiers rode one of the animals—a horse—and herded the others—sheep.

When Coronado demanded that the Zuni swear loyalty to the king of Spain, they replied with arrows. Yet the Zuni were no match for the Spanish soldiers. Their village was captured within the hour, and other Zuni villages soon fell to the Spanish. Coronado's expedition took what they wanted from the pueblos and the people who lived there. When the Zuni tried to defend themselves, the violence against them only increased, leading to the massacre of a large number of Native Americans. People who survived were thrust into slavery.

Coronado and others explored the Southwest, traveling through New Mexico and Texas, reaching as far as Kansas. They brought cattle, sheep, and horses. They introduced new irrigation techniques and created ranches. Most of all, they claimed all the land they crossed in the name of Spain, overpowering anyone who disagreed.

By 1629, the Spanish missionaries had established a Catholic mission at the Zuni village of Hawikku. The Zuni were friendly with the missionaries, and for the most part, hostilities ceased until the Pueblo Revolt of 1680.

HORSES IN NATIVE AMERICAN SOCIETY

While historical images of Native Americans often include horses, this animal didn't originate in America or with Native Americans. One debated theory is that Norse explorers brought horses to North America long ago. More likely, conquistadors like Cortez brought horses when they explored North America. When the Spanish started the New Mexico rancheros in Santa Fe and Taos, thousands of horses came with them. Although the Spanish forbid Native Americans to own horses, the native people who worked on the rancheros soon learned to handle the magnificent animals.

In 1680, the Pueblo Revolt forced Spain out of New Mexico in such a hurry that many horses were left behind. The Native Americans of the Southwest used the horses but also traded them with Plains tribes to the north. Soon wild horses called mustangs became part of the Southwest landscape. "Mustang" comes from "mesteño," Spanish for "stray horse." Today, mustangs still run free in several western states and are protected from harm through the passage of Wild Free-Roaming Horse and Burros Act of 1971.

The Hopi

Like Coronado, Don Juan Oñate took land throughout the Southwest in the name of Spain, including Hopi land in northern Arizona. The Hopi called themselves Hopitu, meaning "peaceful ones." They had farmed northern Arizona since long before the Spanish arrived. Hopi had lived in Oraibi, a village on the Third Mesa, since 1050. As desert dwellers, the Hopi remained concerned about water for crops and daily needs. The Hopi snake dance was (and continues to be) a ritual to ask the snakes to carry prayers of rain to the gods of the underworld. The snake dance is performed by members of the Snake and Antelope clans.

Sharing a close relationship to the land, the Hopi believe their mission is to protect the Earth. Much of Hopi culture centered around the growing and celebrating of corn. Corn is more than just nourishment for the Hopi, it is also a part of their belief system. According to legends, when people came to this world, a kachina or spirit called Maasawu offered them corn. Everyone grabbed the corn, leaving the shortest ear for the Hopi. This short ear of corn taught the Hopi to be humble. Being close to the Earth led to their belief that the Hopi were here to protect the land.

Hopi beliefs state that after making humans, the creator created corn from human flesh, so that the two are always connected. It is a tradition that newborn babies stay in a dark room with their mothers for the first 20 days of life. On the twenty-first day, the baby saw the sun for the first time. After the mother gifted the sun with cornmeal, the baby received an ear of corn called the "corn mother," which was kept for life.

Due the importance of corn in Hopi society, it was important that crops not fail. The Hopi people have always lived in the arid desert climate of Arizona. This type of climate makes farming difficult. Yet by using irrigation and terrace gardening techniques, some of which have been in use since 1200, the Hopi have been successful farmers.

In 1970, a Hopi elder, Dan Katchongva, recorded some of the Hopi prophecies that guided his people. One of these was the "Arrival of Another Race Foretold." Long before the Europeans invaded the land of the native people of the Americas, Hopi elders knew from stone tablets and the rock writings or petroglyphs that another race of people would someday appear and claim the land as their own. This other race "would use force in an attempt to trap us into using weapons, but we must not fall for this trick, for then we ourselves would be brought to our knees, from which we might not be able to rise. Nor must we ever raise our hand against any nation."

Hopi snake dancer.

19

Hopi land wasn't just at risk from this other race that they called the Bahanna. By the early 18th century, the Diné (Navajo) had migrated into the Southwest. The Diné, Spanish, and later Americans remained a threat to the Hopi, who had lived in villages on the top of mesas for hundreds of years.

Meanwhile, the Spanish discovered a much more effective weapon than guns against the Native Americans: smallpox. While most Euro-peans had developed a natural immunity to it, the native people throughout the Americas had no resistance to the disease. It struck with a vengeance, killing many thousands and wiping out entire villages. Some consider the deliber-ate introduction of smallpox to Native Ameri-can communities a form of genocide.

The Texas Missions

SPANISH EXPLORERS never did find their trea-sure, but Catholic missionaries and Span-ish priests often remained behind to build missions and convert Native Americans to Christianity. San Antonio, Texas, was one of the locations where the mission system flour-ished in the 1700s. Five missions were built around the winding San Antonio River: Mis-sion Concepción, Mission San José, Mission San Juan, Mission Espada, and Mission San Antonio de Valero.

Local peaceful bands, collectively called the Coahuiltecans, lived throughout southern Texas and even across the Rio Grande into Coa-huila in northeastern Mexico. In the San Anto-nio area, bands lived in brush huts near the river. They gathered fruits and wild plants and planted gardens with digging sticks. The men hunted with bows and arrows, mainly deer, but occasionally bison, rabbits, and birds. When

SMALLPOX

Smallpox is a highly infectious disease caused by the Variola virus and often transmitted through direct contact, although cases have also been reported from contaminated clothing or bedding. Its name comes from the Latin word for "spotted," which is *pox*. This is what small-pox looks like—a rash of many small, raised bumps.

Smallpox has been around for thousands of years and has caused many deaths. Long ago, smallpox killed up to half its victims and left survivors with deep scars. This disease was espe-cially devastating to Native Americans as they had no natural immunity to the disease. During the French-Indian War (1754–63), the commanding general of the British forces was rumored to have given smallpox-infected blankets to Native American nations that supported the French. In 1781, hundreds of the Piegan Blackfeet people lost their lives to smallpox. Smallpox continued to ravage Native American communities throughout the 1800s. In another epidemic in 1836–37, the Piegan Blackfeet lost two-thirds of their population.

In 1980, smallpox was declared officially eradicated from the world. The last case of small-pox in the United States was in 1949.

needed, they supplemented their diet with lizards and snakes.

The Coahuiltecans also used nets for fishing. The abundant food was often stored in baskets. The large amounts of food and temperate climate made the area an ideal place to live, except for attacks from warring nomadic people, such as the Comanche.

When the Spanish came, the Coahuiltecans aligned with them for protection from the Comanche, but as with other native groups, many died from smallpox. They lived in the missions, which were walled communities where people slept, ate, and learned about Christianity. In return, the Coahuiltecans worked at spinning thread and making soap in workshops within the compound. Other natives worked on the farms outside of the compound or built the aqueducts used for irrigation. Some learned new trades such as blacksmithing, carpentry, masonry, and weaving.

Some native people adjusted to the changes by mixing their traditions with those of the Spanish. Others moved out of the missions when hunting and gathering was plentiful, but moved back in when the food supply dwindled. Still, the warring Comanche remained a fearsome enemy as they tried to drive the Spanish from areas where the Comanche lived and hunted. Comanche and Apache raids successfully destroyed some

missions and limited settlement throughout the Southwest.

Other native communities were also faced with Spanish missionaries who wanted to convert them to Catholicism. The last of the missions was Nuestra Señora Del Refugio, founded in 1793 to focus on coastal bands living along the Gulf of Mexico. The Karankawa people assisted in choosing the site of the mission near Matagorda Bay. The Spanish called the mission the "Place of Refuge." There were only 145 recorded baptisms of Native Americans in more than 30 years, and the mission was finally abandoned in 1830. Twenty years later, the Karan-

(ABOVE) Mission Concepción. (BELOW) Local native people lived at San Jose Mission in Texas

The Three Sisters Garden

NOT ALL Native American tribes were hunters and gatherers. Many were farmers who liked to grow starchy vegetables such as corn, beans, and squash. These were called the "three sisters." Corn is the oldest sister who stands in the center. Squash is the sister who protects the soil with her leaves. The third sister is beans, which grow through the leaves of squash, wrapping themselves around the oldest sister of corn.

Materials
- Soil
- Mulch
- Water
- Corn seeds
- Hoe
- Pole bean seeds
- Squash seeds

A traditional way of growing these vegetables was to plant them together on a small hill of soil. In the spring, prepare a round, flat-topped mound about 3 feet across and 10 to 12 inches high. Remove any weeds, and cover with mulch to keep the hill moist.

In late spring, plant six to eight corn seeds about an inch deep in the middle of the hill, placing them about six inches apart. Water well, and look for corn to sprout in two weeks.

After the corn has sprouted, loosen the soil around the base of the corn stalks using a hoe. Sow approximately a dozen pole bean seeds in a circle around the corn. Look for beans to sprout in another two weeks. Wrap the vines from the beans around the corn stalks when they become long enough.

A week after the beans sprout, plant six to eight squash seeds an inch deep in a circle about a foot outside the circle of beans. Water well, and watch for the squash to sprout in a week. As the squash vines grow larger, turn them to the center of the mound.

kawa band also ceased to exist, mostly likely due to smallpox and other diseases. Native Americans living in missions were particularly at risk of European diseases.

Some Native American nations, such as the Wichita and their allies, the Waco, were able to avoid the dangers of Spanish mission life altogether. Long a fixture on the southern plains, Wichita villages could be found from southern Kansas to northern Texas more than 500 years before the Spanish stepped on North American soil. Accomplished farmers of the "Three Sisters" crops of beans, corn, and squash, the Wichita also left their villages of grass lodges to hunt for bison.

California Indians

SPAIN SETTLED in California much later than in Texas, due to its location farther north and west than the other territories. Hundreds of thousands of Native Americans speaking well over 100 different languages called the region home, some for as long as 10,000 years. Limited from contact with the native people of the Southwest and the Plains due to mountains, desert, and distance, California's native population lived a different kind of life. California was a paradise with temperate weather and plentiful food—fish could be found in the ocean, lakes, and rivers, and edible plants were abundant.

For people like the Chumash, life revolved around the sea, particularly the channel islands near Santa Barbara, although they occasionally traveled to the mountains to gather acorns and piñon nuts. The Chumash felt a strong affinity for the ocean. Early Chumash rock paintings often included images of the dolphin. They became expert at building boats, which they used for travel along the coast or riding with the dolphins.

When not gathering food or making boats, the Chumash lived in domed houses made of willow and reinforced with whalebone. The name Chumash is believed to mean "bead-maker" or "seashell people," but to the Chumash they were the "first people." The Chumash were not a single nation, but actually 75 to 100 communities who spoke one of at least four related languages.

Sadly, European diseases attacked and killed so many that the Chumash were forced to seek help from the Spanish missions.

California's Wappo lived a little farther inland than the Chumash, and they depended upon the Napa River for their livelihood. Living in pole houses in large villages, this hunter-gatherer tribe made their spears and sharp points from obsidian, a type of glass made from the lava of volcanoes. They often used clam-

shell beads as money to buy things. The Wappo were recognized for their basketry skills. Not only were the beautiful baskets decorated with clam shells and abalone, but they could also hold water.

California was a big land, and not all native people lived by the ocean. Other people, such as the Modoc and Shasta, made their homes in the mountains, where they hunted all types of animals.

The 1775 Revolt at Mission San Diego

WHEN THE Spanish arrived and set up a military post in San Diego in 1769, they had been forcing Native Americans into slavery

A Wappo woman.

DEATH OF A LANGUAGE

One of the dangers of assimilation, or merging with a larger population, that the Spanish, and later Americans, insisted on was the abandonment of native languages. Chumashan languages were a group of at least four languages with different dialects. But by the 20th century, most Chumash spoke Spanish or English. The last person who fluently spoke Chumashan died in 1964. Yet linguists, anthropologists, and modern Chumash are working to keep the Chumashan languages alive. Chumashan language dictionaries have been created, and the University of California at Berkeley has been involved in teaching and preserving them.

for over 200 years. The Spanish had few worries about the peaceful California tribes after conquering many Native American bands in New Mexico, Arizona, and Texas.

What started as a trade relationship soon changed to one of forcing Christianity on the native people. Spanish missionaries began trying to convert the Kumeyaay people like they had many California natives. The Spanish failed to recognize the increasing tensions as the Kumeyaay resisted their efforts to change their culture. The religion of area Native Americans involved dancing, sometimes with masks. The Spanish priests viewed these activities as demonic and demanded they stop.

The mission moved closer to the native villages in 1774, and missionaries used stronger tactics to convert Native Americans, baptizing almost 400 in two months' time. Many Kumeyaay feared and avoided the priests, who they believed to be powerful shamans.

Spanish soldiers caused other problems when they committed violence against native women and stole food. On top of this, the European diseases killed 78 out of every 1,000 Native Americans in California. All of these things, plus forced labor in the mission fields, pushed many California natives to the edge.

The tensions boiled over in 1775, and natives from 15 villages raided the San Diego mission where eleven Spanish people lived. One of the priests intent on converting as many California Indians as possible, Father Luis Jayme, was one of three killed.

The Spanish reaction to the revolt was one of stunned disbelief. They thought that the California Indians, unlike those in the Southwest, were peaceful and agreeable. The Spanish were clueless about the problems their presence had caused.

After the rebellion, the Spanish clamped down. Any outbreaks among Native Americans at the missions were quickly subdued. European diseases had already weakened many tribes. The Spanish also introduced livestock and seed crops that crowded out the game animals and plants

Native Americans in the missions made baskets and spun ropes from hair.

Weaving

STYLES OF weaving and basketry varied among Native American nations. California bands such as the Pomo and Washoe valued a tightly woven basket that could carry food and even water. Baskets were typically made from nearby plant material, which might be grass, wheat, reeds, or other products. You can also make a basket out of available materials. Newspaper is a good choice because it's readily available, plus it is a good way to recycle.

Materials
◆ Newspaper
◆ Craft glue

Fold each sheet of newspaper in half. Unfold, and from each side begin folding toward the center so that each fold is the same width (1 inch to 1½ inch is a good width).

Continue folding from each side until the sides meet in the center. You might want to glue the final fold together.

Lay out four of the newspaper strips, two across each way so that they intersect. Weave each strip in and out of the strips in the opposite direction. Do this several times until you have the bottom of your basket. The weaving should be centered on the newspaper strips, making a square. Leave the

ends of the strips sticking out—two strips in each of the four directions.

Bend the ends of the strips to point up. Take a new strip of newspaper and weave it in and out of

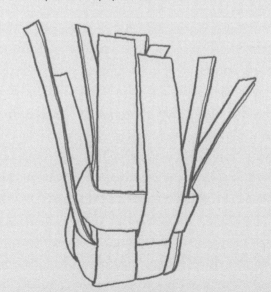

the strips coming from the base. When you near the end of a horizontal strip, either tuck it in securely to one of the vertical strips or use glue to attach it.

Continue weaving the sides with additional newspaper strips until you reach the desired height. Use one last strip (or two, if needed) to fold over the top of the basket to hold it secure. Glue this last strip in place as the top rim.

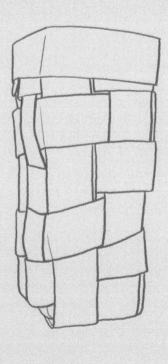

Tell a Story

"I AM going to tell stories of the old days now. All of you lie down and stretch out on your backs, otherwise you will be humpbacked, my father used to say. Then he would tell stories and teach us."

Native Americans have a long history of storytelling. More than entertainment, traditional storytelling preserves information about cultures and traditions. Because Ishi shared stories of his people, knowledge about the Yahi culture is preserved. Many traditional stories explain why and how the animals and people came to be. Other stories tell a message. Instead of lecturing a person who is conceited about her long, beautiful hair, a traditional storyteller might tell the story of the possum with the thick, furry tail. Possum's friends became so tired of hearing Possum talk about his tail that they tricked him into putting a special medicine on it. The medicine loosened the hair, leaving the tail bare and ugly. The lesson from the story is to beware of being too vain or you might lose your "beautiful tail" too.

Now it's your turn. Create a story with at least one animal as the main character. Make your story entertaining, but make sure it has a message as well.

that the native people depended on for food. Hogs began to run wild and eat the abundance of acorns that provided protein to the Native Americans. Those who didn't flee California found themselves forced into the missions, where they were expected to work hard for the Spanish. Parents and children were separated. Entire California bands disappeared as approximately one-third of the state's Native Americans died as a result of the mission system.

The Decimation of California Tribes

By 1820, more than 20,000 of the remaining Native Americans lived in slavery at California missions. Over 90 percent of the largely coastal native populations were gone by 1848. After California became a state in 1850, the abuses continued. One of the first laws was the 1850 Act for the Government and Protection of Indians, which removed Native Americans from traditional lands and broke up families. With this law, California legally turned native people, including children, into slaves through apprenticing or indenturing them to the white population. Homeless people were arrested. If they couldn't pay their bail, they were punished by being placed at a public auction and sold to the highest bidder.

The California Constitution allowed the governor to order sheriffs on "expeditions against the Indians." White men were appointed as Indian agents to take charge of the remaining Native Americans, and many allowed more people to die. Not all Indian agents were deceitful; some, such as Superintendent of the California Indian Agency E. G. Beale, spoke out against how Native Americans were treated. Fearful of the planned extinction of California's natives, he made a plea in 1852.

Driven from their fishing and hunting grounds, hunted themselves like wild beasts, lassoed, and torn from homes made miserable by want, and forced into slavery, the wretched remnant which escapes starvation on the one hand, and the relentless whites on the other, only do so to rot and die of a loathsome disease, the penalty of Indian association with frontier civilization.... It is a crying sin that our government, so wealthy and so powerful, should shut its eyes to the miserable fate of these rightful owners of the soil.

When they addressed Congress in 1904, the Northern California Indian Association said, "[I]t is doubtful if there is any people in America, even on the East Side of New York City, whose presence is so miserable or whose future is so appalling as some of the Indian bands in northern California; for we have here not only the squalor of the present, but a hopelessness of despair unknown even in the slums of darkest New York."

Ishi

MANY NATIVE American bands ceased to exist as the last members of tribes or bands died. Many suffered the fate of Ishi, known as the last Yahi Indian of California.

Born around 1860, Ishi wandered into a northern California town called Oroville in 1911. His hair was short; he had burned it off when the last of his family had died. Cutting your hair when someone you loved or had ties to died was not only a Yahi mourning custom, but a custom of several other Native American bands or nations as well.

At first, the townspeople didn't know what to do with this sad-looking Indian man. He couldn't speak English, and they couldn't speak Yahi. He was put in jail and given food. An anthropologist, T. T. Waterman, came to see Ishi. Waterman knew some Yana words, a different dialect from the same language fam-

ily. When Ishi recognized some of the words, Waterman brought Ishi to the University of California Museum of Anthropology. He arranged for a man of the Yana band to help interpret.

It was against Yahi custom to tell your name, so the anthropologists named him Ishi, which means "man" in Yana. Ishi lived in the museum. He was recorded telling stories and singing songs so that his language could be preserved. He also demonstrated how to make arrow points to the public. Anthropologists today believe that Ishi may have had a mixed heritage that included Wintu or Nomlaki because his arrow points more closely resembled those of those bands.

Ishi was also exposed to a different type of life in San Francisco. Anthropologists reported that he seemed most impressed by the large crowds of people. The wife of one of the anthropologists who learned from Ishi, Theodora Kroeber, wrote Ishi's story in *Ishi in Two Worlds: A Biography of the Last Wild Indian in North America*.

In 1914, Ishi took anthropologists Waterman and Alfred Kroeber to his home at Deer Creek. Soon afterward, Ishi developed tuberculosis. Five years after entering Oroville, Ishi died on March 25, 1916, the last of the Yahi.

Ishi.

3

EUROPEANS SETTLE
on the EASTERN SHORE

O**NE OF** the first stories many people hear about Native Americans is the Pilgrims' arrival in 1620. After a difficult year, the new settlers and their Indian neighbors celebrated with a feast, thus starting the American tradition of Thanksgiving.

In 1970 Frank James, a member of the Wampanoag tribe that had befriended the Pilgrims, was asked to speak at the 350th anniversary of the Europeans' arrival in America. To James and many others, the Thanksgiving holiday was a time of sorrow. The Wampanoag had welcomed these new people and helped them adjust, yet within 50 years of their meeting, the Wampanoag were almost wiped out by guns and diseases brought by the new settlers.

It was a tale repeated often between Native American nations and European Americans in the United States. Europeans from England, France, the Netherlands, and other countries began arriving on the East Coast in large numbers during the 1600s. At the time, two language groups of Native Americans were the primary inhabitants of the Northeast, the region that would become the original 13 colonies. They were the Algonquian-speaking people and the Iroquois-speaking people.

Algonquian People of the Eastern Woodlands

THE ALGONQUIAN (also spelled Algonkian) people spoke different dialects of the same language. One tribe of that group was the Wampanoag, which means "Eastern People," and included dozens of subtribes or bands. The Wampanoag lived primarily in wigwams—round-roofed houses covered in elm or birch bark—throughout Massachusetts and Rhode Island. Each Wampanoag village operated independently with a leader called a *sachem* and a tribal council. Similar to today's mayors and city councils, the sachem and council made the important decisions.

In spring, the Wampanoag fished in the rivers for herring and salmon. They planted gardens of maize, or corn, plus other vegetables. People hunted during the summer and autumn—deer, beaver, otter, and bear. These animals not only provided the Wampanoag with food, but also clothing from the skins and tools from the bones.

Among the Wampanoag, respect was very important. They respected the animals around them. When they made a kill, they left an offering of bones or meat to the Creator or other deity in the belief system of the specific tribe. Respect to neighbors and visitors included sharing whatever food they had, even if they only had a little.

When the Pilgrims landed on the rocky shores of Cape Cod in 1620, it wasn't the first time the Wampanoag had seen white people. Other Europeans had sailed along the eastern coast in the 1500s, most notably the French and English. In 1564, French Protestants established a colony near Jacksonville, Florida, at Fort Caroline, although it was later taken over by the Spanish. The first British colony had already been established at Jamestown, Virginia, in 1607.

The Wampanoag became used to seeing European fishing boats, and sometimes traded corn and furs with these foreign people. One of the Wampanoag was a Patuxet man named Tisquantum, who had most likely met one of the Jamestown leaders, Captain John Smith. Tisquantum, who became known as Squanto, also met a different kind of sea captain, Thomas Hunt. To make his trips to the New World more profitable, Hunt seized Native Americans to sell as slaves. In 1614, Captain Hunt captured some Wampanoag, including Tisquantum, to sell to the Spanish.

Tisquantum later gained his freedom from Spanish monks and made his way to England, where he learned the language and customs of the British. In 1619 he signed on as an interpreter on an expedition to Newfoundland, Canada. Back in North America, Tisquantum made his way south to his village, only to learn that everyone there had died from an epidemic, perhaps smallpox. With no family or village, Tisquantum lived with other Wampanoag nearby.

After the success of the Jamestown colony, another group of English settlers arrived in Cape Cod on the *Mayflower* in November 1620. They were the Pilgrims, who left England to escape religious persecution. But they were

An early Algonquian portrait.

MAIZE

Better known today as corn, maize figured heavily in Mayan culture and in the oral history of many native people in the Americas. It is believed to have started as a wild plant, teocinte, but evolved into the cultivated maize of Mexico and Central America. From there, maize spread both north and south, and was eventually introduced to Europe by Christopher Columbus.

Many cultures ground up the maize to make bread products for eating. Some native groups also used maize in ceremonies and offerings. The Hopi, in particular, have historically prized maize. Today, corn is one of the most widely grown vegetables in the United States and the world.

THE TRUE STORY OF JOHN SMITH AND POCAHONTAS

The legend of Pocahontas and John Smith has long been told as a romantic tale between two adults. Instead, it was a friendship that began with a girl of 10 or 12 years old. Pocahontas, the daughter of a chief named Powhatan, was a friendly and spirited girl who met John Smith and other colonists when they arrived in Jamestown in 1607. When Smith was captured by Powhatan's warriors in late 1607, he felt certain he faced death as several natives stood over him with clubs. But Pocahontas rushed in, and according to Smith, she took his "head in her arms and laid her owne upon his to save him from death."

Afterward, Pocahontas often visited Jamestown to deliver food and talk with her friend John Smith. In 1609, Smith was injured by gunpowder. He returned to England, and Pocahontas was told that Smith had died. Another Jamestown colonist, Captain Samuel Argall, kidnapped Pocahontas and held her for ransom. When Powhatan refused to pay the entire ransom, Pocahontas remained at English settlements, learning the customs and Christianity. At her baptism, she took the name Rebecca.

Pocahontas met a tobacco farmer named John Rolfe, whom she married in 1614. She, her husband, and a son sailed to London in 1616. She was presented to King James I and was very popular with the British public. But perhaps the best part of her trip was being reunited with John Smith, who hadn't died after all. She insisted on addressing him as "father."

When Pocahontas and her family decided to return home to Virginia in early 1617, she fell ill from either pneumonia or tuberculosis. She died at the age of 22.

unprepared for a New England winter. A small party sent ahead to explore this new land stumbled into a Nauset cemetery, but all the starving Pilgrims noticed was the baskets of corn. Leaving baskets of food as an offering to the dead was a Nauset custom. The Pilgrims began to take the corn, but Nauset warriors showed up and ran them off.

The Pilgrims then found a deserted village on the other side of the bay, which they made their home. The Wampanoag had moved their villages inland to protect themselves from the cold north winds, living off the food they had saved for winter. With little food and poor shelter, half of the Pilgrims died during the first winter.

The Wampanoag watched the starving Europeans for months and determined that they probably weren't a threat. In March a sachem from an Algonquian band called the Abenaki entered Plymouth, saying, "Hello, Englishmen." The sachem was Samoset, and he had learned English from British fishermen and traders. After reviewing the Pilgrims' situation, he left and returned with Tisquantum.

The village where the Pilgrims spent their winter was Tisquantum's old village, Patuxet. As a Wampanoag, Tisquantum had been raised to help others. He taught the Pilgrims skills to survive, such as how to plant crops that would grow on the rocky ground. Tisquantum even mediated peace between the English and the Pokanoket Wampanoag band that lived nearby.

In that first treaty of friendship, Massasoit, the Pokanoket sachem, gave the Pilgrims use of 12,000 acres for their settlement. Native American concepts of owning land differed from those of the Europeans. Most Indians believed that you couldn't own the land. Everyone in a tribe or nation was entitled to use the

Samoset greets an Englishman at the Plymouth settlement.

land. When making treaties, Native American leaders were granting the Europeans use of the land, not personal ownership.

The Pokanoket also hoped that the new settlers would be allies with them against their enemies, the Narragansett. The illness that had wiped out the Patuxet village had devastated many Wampanoag bands, including the Pokanoket. This left them vulnerable to enemies.

After that first year, the Pilgrims showed their gratitude by inviting the Wampanoag to a celebration: Thanksgiving. The number of Wampanoag overwhelmed the Pilgrim's meager supply of food, so Massasoit's band brought five deer, wild turkey, corn, squash, and berries for the three-day celebration. The leader of the Pilgrims, Miles Standish, sat at one end of the table, and Massasoit sat on the other end.

Tisquantum continued to live among the English, serving as an interpreter. Later, Massasoit became very angry with Tisquantum, who he believed was trying to mislead both the Pokanoket and the Pilgrims. But Tisquantum died from an illness, two years after meeting the Pilgrims.

The friendship between Massasoit and the Pilgrims lasted for the remainder of Massasoit's life. The colonists even nursed Massasoit back to health when he became ill in the winter of 1623. However, things were changing. The settlers often objected to native dress, customs,

Communicate Without Speaking

NATIVE AMERICANS didn't speak English before the British came to America, nor did the British speak any of the many Native American languages. Eventually, some people learned, but until they could, communication was difficult. How would you communicate with someone with whom you didn't share the same language?

Make up important information (not just a single word or two) that you would like another person to know. Try to communicate that information to the other person without using verbal or written language. What happens? How do you feel?

and religion. It was unfortunate that the Pilgrims, who had experienced religious persecution, could be so intolerant of other religions.

Later settlers, mainly English and Dutch, were better prepared for starting a life in a new land. Strong trading relationships developed between the Algonquian people and Europeans, particularly the Dutch West India Company. One of these bands was the Lenni Lenape (Delaware), who traded an island, later called Manhattan, to the Dutch.

The Pequot War (1636–38)

WHEN RELATIONSHIPS weren't built upon the mutual benefit of trading, the situation between the native people and the colonists worsened. Colonists, particularly the English Puritans, took the land they wanted and captured native people as slaves. Eventually the Pequot of Connecticut, who had already lost half of their people to smallpox and had not signed any treaties or agreements with the colonists, fought back against the Europeans.

The Pequot War was the first war between colonists and native people. Skirmishes began as early as 1634 as the Pequot tried to regain trading rights lost to other tribes by attacking Narragansett people trading at a Dutch fort. The Dutch retaliated by kidnapping and killing a Grand Sachem. Later, an English pirate kidnapped sev-

A painting shows the Wampanog and Pilgrims sharing food at the first Thanksgiving.

A battle in the Pequot War.

34

eral Pequot and held them for ransom. Again, the Pequot retaliated against the English.

The battles continued until May of 1637 when the Pequot had gathered for their annual Green Corn Festival. Many English and Dutch colonists surrounded the native people as they slept. When the Pequot awakened, they were ordered outside. As the men exited the dwelling, they were killed by guns and clubs. Fires were set to approximately 80 dwellings, killing the women and children who remained inside. Approximately 600 died. The surviving Pequot were sold into slavery or went to live with neighboring Wampanoag bands. Their descendants spent more than 300 years trying to get their land back. The Mashantucket Pequot reached their goal in 1983, when they finally received federal recognition and a reservation.

The Pequot War was the first of many wars between Europeans and Native Americans in New England. Wamsutta, Massasoit's son, became sachem after Massasoit's death in 1660. Wamsutta was more independent than his father, which worried the colonists. After the colonists invited him to Plymouth for talks, Wamsutta died of suspected poisoning.

King Philip's War

WAMSUTTA'S BROTHER, Metacomet, became the next leader of the Pokanoket. As the colonists continued taking land and tried to force the remaining natives onto reservations, the Pokanoket became angered at the English. Metacomet had grown up around

THE FIRST RESERVATION

When the Puritans settled in what would become New Haven, Connecticut, they met an Algonquian band that they called the Quinnipiac. The Quinnipiac, already weakened by disease, numbered only 250 to 300 people. The Quinnipiac sachems signed a treaty with the Puritans on November 24, 1638. That treaty included establishing or reserving land for the Quinnipiac on the east side of the harbor. But life there continued to be difficult. While some may have joined other Native American nations, the Quinnipiac are believed to have ceased existing as a separate nation past the American Revolution.

the Pilgrims and even had an English name. He was known as King Philip among the settlers. Metacomet looked among other Wampanoag for support against the colonists. John Sassamon, who served as Metacomet's secretary for about 10 years, warned the Plymouth leaders of Wampanoag plans to attack the colonists. Soon, Sassamon was found dead, and the Pilgrims tried and executed three Wampanoag for Sassamon's murder.

Tired of abuse and trickery from the colonists, many Wampanoag bands joined forces against the English under the leadership of Metacomet. The warriors first attacked the town of Swansea in Plymouth Colony in June 1675 after a Wampanoag was killed there. They moved on to the northern settlements and burned some of the towns. As Metacomet gained allies among other Wampanoag bands, the conflict known as King Philip's War spread throughout New England.

At the beginning, it looked liked the Wampanoag might win. Except for a colonial victory at the Great Swamp in Rhode Island, Metacomet's forces had been successful. Yet as the conflicts multiplied, the limited Wampanoag forces

As sachem of the Wampanoag, Metacomet (known as King Philip to the whites) discussed a treaty with the settlers.

began faltering. Outnumbered by the colonists, the Wampanoag suffered from the lack of food and ammunition. The colonists also gained help from other Native Americans, such as the Mohawk, who sided with them. After more than a year of fighting, Wampanoag forces retreated.

The English colonists fought with a vengeance, burning many of the Wampanoag villages that they came across. They also left strong messages behind. When Wamsutta's widow drowned during an escape, the colonists cut off her head and displayed it in the town. An informer, John Alderman, led forces to Metacomet before shooting and killing the noted sachem. Alderman was given one of Metacomet's hands as a trophy. Metacomet's head was put on a pole in Plymouth, where it remained for 25 years as a grisly message to other Native Americans. Metacomet's nine-year-old son was captured and imprisoned. After some debate among the colonists, he was sent to the West Indies as a slave.

Although the war more or less ended with Metacomet's death, it would take another two years before a peace treaty was signed. Until that happened, the British hunted down Metacomet's allies until the Wampanoag were almost exterminated.

The deadly conflict between the colonists and the Algonquian people devastated the colonies, but the native people of the area paid the greatest price. Entire families were sold into slavery. Others escaped by fleeing to Canada. Some Wampanoag refused to leave their home and adapted to living among the colonists. In less than 100 years, only 400 Wampanoag survived the epidemics, conflicts, and wars, of the 12,000 Wampanoag who had lived in New England in 1600.

Today, the Wampanoag Nation, established in 1928, includes five bands of about 3,000 people. Only the Gay Head Wampanoag are a federally recognized band.

The Iroquois (Haudenosaunee) Confederacy

DURING THE first wave of European immigration, the Iroquoian language family was the other primary Native American language group in New England. This broad group, which spoke many dialects, ranged from Canadian natives down to the Cherokee of North Carolina. But ultimately, there were only five (and later six) nations that belonged to the Iroquois Confederacy.

As with many Native American names used to identify a band or tribe, the Iroquois received the name they are known by from the Algonquian people. "Iroquois" comes from an Algonquian word meaning "Real Adders."

An adder is a snake, and the Algonquian and Iroquois people were often at war with each other. The people of the Five Nations referred to themselves as Haudenosaunee, which translates to "People of the Longhouse." When the English and French first settled New England, the Iroquois or Haudenosaunee people were a strong group of five Indian nations—Cayuga, Mohawk, Oneida, Onondaga, and Seneca—and were often referred to as the Five Indian Nations, or just Five Nations.

The People of the Longhouse had a long history before the Europeans. They referred to America as the Great Island or Turtle Island. In their origin story, the world developed upon the back of a giant turtle. According to David Cusick, a Tuscarora painter and physician, five families once lived in the mountains where they battled serpents and monsters. Cusick put the Haudenosaunee origin story to paper in 1826 or 1827 in *David Cusick's Sketches of Ancient History of the Six Nations*: "Perhaps 1,000 years before Columbus discovered ... America, ... [a]bout the time the Five Families become independent nations, ... they formed Council fire in each nation."

Most people of the Five Nations lived in longhouses. These long wood homes, some as large as football fields, were the homes of clans related through the females. There were nine clans in all: Turtle, Wolf, Deer, Bear, Hawk, Heron, Beaver, Snipe, and Eel. When a couple married, the husband moved in with his wife's family. The longhouse was not only their home, but also a symbol of how the Five Nation Confederacy lived. Between the roof (sky) and the floor (earth) lived the fires (Five Nations).

People of the Five Nations had been living in longhouses for at least 700 years when the Europeans arrived. As many as 20 families might live in a longhouse with several longhouses making up a village. Some larger villages held

The original Five Nations.

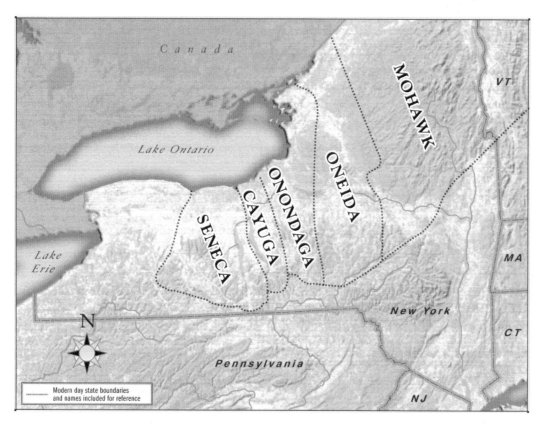

Modern day state boundaries and names included for reference

Build a Native American Community

IROQUOIS LIVED in longhouses, and Plains tribes lived in tepees. Other Native Americans lived in wigwams, log cabins, and plank houses. Many different types of Native American housing existed in North America in the 1600s and 1700s. Each community used housing that fit its lifestyle.

Some tribes were agricultural—they lived in settled villages and farmed the land for corn and vegetables. They wanted houses that would last a long time. Other tribes were more nomadic, moving frequently from place to place as they hunted and gathered food and resources. They needed houses that were portable or easy to build.

Since North America is such a big continent with different climates, different tribes had very different weather to contend with. In the Arizona deserts, temperatures could hit 120° Fahrenheit, and in the Alaskan tundra, –50° F was not unusual. Naturally, Native Americans developed different types of dwellings to survive in such different environments.

Research how a specific tribe lived hundreds of years ago, and re-create a specific type of community. Some examples of Native American villages/communities include: Iroquois (longhouses), Plains people (tepees), Pueblo and ancient Puebloans (adobe), Southeastern tribes such as the Cherokee (wattle and daub; log cabins), Northwestern people (plank houses), Algonquian and Southern Plains (wigwams), Navajo and some Plains nations (earth lodges), and Inuit (igloos).

Materials

- ◆ Particle board or thick cardboard to serve as a base for the community
- ◆ Glue
- ◆ Scissors

Craft material for making houses: craft sticks, grass, small sticks or twigs, construction paper, felt in appropriate colors

Here are some suggested Web sites to get you started:

www.mnsu.edu/emuseum/prehistory/
   settlements
www.native-languages.org/houses.htm
www.greatdreams.com/native/nativehsg.htm

Look around your home for other odds and ends that you could use to make your Native American community. Use your imagination.

Play Ball-and-Triangle

AS WITH other cultures, Native Americans had favorite games that they enjoyed playing. Penobscot children who lived in the New England area once played Ball-and-Triangle. The game used a triangular piece of birch bark with a hole cut in the center. A string was attached to one corner of the bark. The other end of the string was attached to the ball. The object of the game was to swing the ball up, and then make it drop through the hole. Make your own Ball-and-Triangle game and invite some friends to play.

Materials
◆ Cardboard
◆ Scissors
◆ Ruler
◆ Small rubber ball
◆ 18-inch long string
◆ Strong tape

Cut the cardboard into the shape of a triangle with each side about 8 to 10 inches long. Trace the ball in the center of the triangle. Cut out a hole slightly larger than the ball so that the ball can pass through it.

Poke a small hole in one corner of the triangle. Insert one end of the string through the hole and tie a knot. Tie the other end of the string around the ball and knot it. Use tape to secure the string to the ball.

To play Ball-and-Triangle, hold one end of the triangle (not the end with the string). Swing the ball upward to let it drop through the center hole. If you can do it, you get a point. Whether you get a point or not, pass the triangle to the next player to try. Continue around the circle of players. The first person to reach 10 points wins the game.

up to 200 longhouses. The Iroquois nations typically used the slash-and-burn method to clear land for villages and farms. Stockades surrounded the villages for protection against surprise attacks. After an area's resources were exhausted, the people in the village found a new location and started building again, usually in the summer months.

The women grew food—corn, squash, beans, and sunflowers—outside the village walls. Occasionally, children and elderly men helped with the farming. The first corn was harvested in late summer for the Green Corn Festival, a type of thanksgiving celebrated by the Five Nations people. The men dug storage pits, lining them with bark and grass. More sheets of bark covered food kept in the storage pits. When not helping with the building, men hunted deer and elk with bow and arrows or fished with spears.

As a group of powerful nations with plentiful food, the Haudenosaunee had free time for storytelling, games such as lacrosse, and music. In addition to singing, the flute and drum were popular instruments. The flute was sometimes used as part of the courtship ritual. If an Iroquois man played the flute outside of a woman's longhouse, it meant that he liked her. The Haudenosaunee also liked to fill their drums with water to create a different sound.

When the colonists began arriving, the Iroquois people controlled large amounts of land in the East, with a large concentration of Confederacy villages found in upstate New York. As larger numbers of French and English moved onto the Iroquois' lands, many villages relocated to Canada in parts of Ontario, Quebec, and Alberta.

Early Europeans did some trading with people of the Five Nations, particularly the Mohawk. The Five Nations traded animal skins, often beaver, for European goods like knives, iron axes, blankets, and clothing. By the 1700s, many Haudenosaunee wore European clothing they adapted for their use. For example, women might add traditional beading to European skirts.

Perhaps what most impressed the colonists most about the Five Nations was their advanced style of government. These nations had political alliances that had successfully served the people in times of war and peace and in matters of trade. According to the oral history of the people, a Huron prophet called the Peacemaker proposed a system of governing in which thinking replaced violence. An Onondaga chief, Hiawatha, carried this message to the different nations. Fifty sachems from the Five Nations met at a Grand Council in the 12th century to form the confederacy of nations.

While each nation had its own tribal council to govern within the nation, they also sent officials to the Grand Council to make decisions that affected the entire confederacy. For governing purposes, the Mohawk and Seneca were one house, or side, and the Cayugas and Oneidas were the other. Each side considered an issue and tried to reach an agreement. If they couldn't settle the matter, it would go to the "Firekeepers"—the Onondagas—for the deciding vote.

LONGHOUSES

When the colonists first saw the longhouses of the Five Nations, they had to be impressed. While only 20 feet wide, the homes ranged from 180 to 220 feet long—more square footage than the average American home today.

A longhouse typically took several days to build if all the families who were to live in it pitched in. These rectangular houses were made of cedar, pine, and elm and could hold hundreds of people. Sheets of bark covered 20-foot-high curved roofs that kept the heat in. The bark, preferably from elm trees, was peeled in the late spring when it was easiest to remove from trees. Sheets of bark removed from elm trees were then laced together with narrow strips of bark from trees like hickory. Strips of bark were flexible when wet and could be threaded through the sheets of bark and latched onto poles. As the bark dried, it shrank and became tight. Longhouses were built with tools made from stones and the bones of animals. Deer hide glue also attached pieces of wood together.

Although longhouses had doorways at each end, there were no windows. A row of fires lined the center of a longhouse, and holes in the roof let the smoke out. Individual family storage units and platforms divided each family's area and allowed some privacy.

A typical village contained a special longhouse where the main sachem lived. Often the longest of the houses, it was also a place for ceremonies and meetings.

The Nations' style of government would influence America's Founding Fathers, such as Benjamin Franklin, to create the United States' legislative bodies of the Senate and House of Representatives. In fact, Franklin invited the Six Nations Confederacy (the Tuscarora joined in 1722) to explain their government at a delegation meeting in Albany, New York. The government of the Six Nations Confederacy was a model for the Articles of Confederation and the Constitution of the United States.

What the United States didn't adopt from the Six Nations was the important leadership role of women in government. The Six Nations had a system of government that was balanced not only between nations, but also between males and females. Male leaders were sachems and served on councils. Native women elected as "clan mothers" were leaders among the nations and had the deciding vote in many issues, as well as deciding who would represent the nation at the Grand Council. The clan mothers also had an influence on American society, particularly the early fight for women's rights at the 1848 Seneca Falls Convention.

Like the Algonquian people, the Six Nations also had difficulties with the colonists, although many early conflicts were with the French instead of the British. The first peace treaty may have been between the French and the Haudenosaunee in 1624. Like most treaties, this one didn't last.

The Six Nations were more successful in their alliances with the English. Unlike many Algonquian nations, the Iroquois actually increased in population in the early 1600s. Located farther inland, they avoided the diseases that devastated the Wampanoag. They

An Iroquois gathering, 1914.

also conquered other Iroquois-speaking people, such as the Huron, and adopted them into the Six Nations.

Yet policies after the American Revolution eventually led to a breakup of many New York villages in the 1800s. Although members of each nation remain in New York, many Oneida moved to Green Bay, Wisconsin. Many of the Cayuga Nation relocated to Ohio and later to Indian Territory (Oklahoma), where today they belong to the Seneca-Cayuga Nation.

The largest population of the original Five Nations is the Mohawk Nation, with approximately 35,000 people. Most Mohawk people live in Canada, although a large number of the Caughnawaga band live in Brooklyn, New York, in addition to a reservation at the New York–Quebec border.

FIGHTING the WHITE MAN'S WARS

WAVE AFTER wave of European settlers arrived on New England's shores in the late 17th and 18th centuries. These new settlers were more likely to take the land than to buy it, and many Native American nations found themselves being pushed west of the Appalachian Mountains.

Conflicts such as the two-year Tuscarora Indian War in North Carolina continued to break out between Native Americans and colonists. Yet more often conflicts broke out between the different European nations— the Swedish against the Dutch, the Dutch against the English, the English against the French, the French against the Spanish. Europeans constantly fought over land; who owned it, and who had trading rights.

Unfortunately, when European conflicts occurred, Native Americans were often affected. Although they could sometimes manipulate the countries against one another, Native Americans were increasingly asked to fight with one country against another.

Many Native American communities tried to remain neutral, yet for the most part only the Haudenosaunee were stable and powerful enough to accomplish this. Other bands and nations were pulled into the conflicts, particularly the French and Indian War that started in 1754. Native Americans quickly learned that punishment came with supporting the losing side.

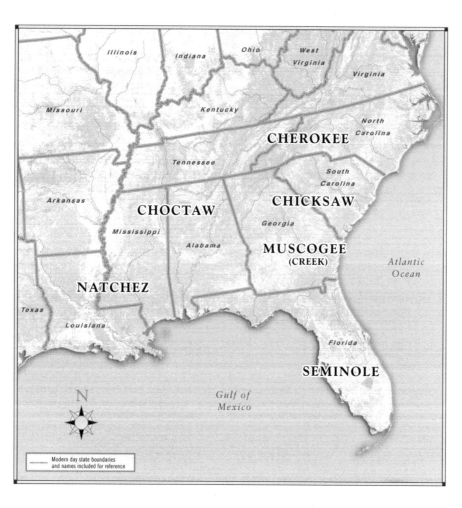

The French and Indian War (1754–63)

DESPITE ITS name, the French and Indian War was really a war between the French and the British over land in the Ohio River Valley. When the fighting extended to Europe it was known as the Seven Years' War. As the first real war fought between European nations in North America, the participation of Native Americans was critical.

Some Native Americans already lived in the Ohio River Valley; others, such as the Iroquois nations and the Delaware, used it as hunting grounds. Yet it became common to see merchants and fur traders from both England and France wandering through Ohio and the western part of Pennsylvania. Some trappers became very friendly with Native American nations, learning the native language and sometimes marrying into a particular band.

Design a Trading Post

TRADING POSTS were important on the western frontier, not unlike the superstores of today. They provided a place to get supplies, a location for Native Americans and trappers to trade goods, and a place to get the latest news. Trading posts were often located near heavily traveled areas. For example, Fort Union Trading Post in North Dakota was located where the Missouri and Yellowstone rivers met. This allowed the post to draw traffic from people riding on horses or boats. Fort Union was also centrally located between several Native American bands or nations. Beaver fur was often traded for goods in the early years; later buffalo hides fetched the highest prices. Goods could be food, blankets, gunpowder, or supplies for the road. A blacksmith might be on site to reshoe a soldier's horse.

Make a diorama of a trading post, making certain to include items that might be found at a trading post. This activity may need supervision during the cutting activities.

Materials

◆ Paper
◆ Pencil
◆ Sturdy cardboard or display board as base
◆ Glue
◆ Cardboard boxes in assorted shapes or sizes
◆ Miniature people and animals
◆ Miniature foodstuffs, landscaping, and/or building elements
◆ Modeling clay
◆ Poster or acrylic paints
◆ Scissors or a craft knife

Choose the scale of your diorama. A typical scale is one inch representing one foot. Sketch a diagram of how you want your diorama to look. Choose and gather the materials you'll need.

First, create the background for your diorama, keeping in mind the environment trading posts existed in during the 1800s. For example, you probably wouldn't find wild animals such as bears or mountain lions in a trading post.

Construct the trading post building and glue it onto the base. The building should be sturdy. It can be made of cardboard, craft sticks, or appropriately sized twigs (to represent logs). Using glue or putty, attach smaller objects you've created into the diorama.

A Navajo trading post.

Both the British and the French saw the region as a place to make money, and English trading posts and French forts sprang up throughout the wilderness.

THE ORIGIN OF SCALPING

People often associate scalping—removing the top part of the skin of the head with the hair—with Native Americans. But the first people known to engage in scalping were Scythians, a group living in southeastern Europe and southwestern Asia from 400 to 800 B.C. Other pre-Columbian sites in North America also showed evidence of scalping, although different methods were used. By the time of European contact in the Americas, scalping was reported among eastern groups like Muskogean, Iroquoian, and Algonquian speaking people.

Scalping, however, increased with the arrival of the Europeans, who encouraged scalping as evidence of a kill. Governor Charles Lawrence (born in Plymouth) decided that the best way to deal with the attacks by area natives in the Canadian territory of Nova Scotia was to issue a "scalp proclamation" in 1756 in

The British pay for scalps.

which the scalp of a male native was worth 25 British pounds—over $3,000 today. The Mexican government also promoted the practice of scalping between 1835 and 1880 by paying a bounty for Native American scalps, particularly the Comanche and Apache.

Many Native Americans welcomed the French fur trappers. The fur trade with these French often benefitted both sides, and native people were typically welcomed at French forts with gifts. It wasn't surprising that many natives sided with the French. Additionally, large numbers of British colonists had been taking native land, and many native people feared that these colonists would continue moving west, forcing them from their land as they had already done in New England.

In 1754, the first battle took place. George Washington's colonial troops attempted to drive the French from the Ohio Valley by capturing Fort Duquesne. When Washington gained the lead in the beginning through a surprise attack, the English erected Fort Necessity. Slightly over a month later, the French struck back and quickly overwhelmed Washington's troops.

The French remained successful in many battles in the early years of the war. The chief reason was their Native American allies. While some Indian nations signed agreements with the British or remained neutral, an increasingly larger number sided with the French, including many of the Algonquian people. At first, the combination of the French and the Native Americans proved almost overwhelming, with war tactics that may have included scalping. Finally, the British decided to put everything they had into winning that war.

The tide turned for the British when the white Americans known as colonials sought similar agreements with Native Americans, such as the Iroquois. In 1758, Brigadier General John Forbes held a council with area Native Americans and established peace. Without their native allies, the French abandoned Fort Duquesne to the British, who renamed it Fort Pitt. Fort Pitt later became the city of Pittsburgh.

The British Americans had often supplied Native American bands with whom they were friendly with food, clothing, seed, and blankets. These supplies were cut off to those Native American nations who fought alongside the French. With the defeat of the French in 1763, the British gained control of the northeastern United States and parts of Canada. The number of colonists reached 1,500,000 and continued to climb. The number of Native Americans began to drop drastically. The Native Americans who fought on the side of the British gained little for their efforts as new colonists began pouring onto native lands when the war with the French ended.

Chief Pontiac of the Ottawa Nation led attacks against the British to drive the colonists away from the Ohio Valley. Pontiac was a brilliant military strategist. With the help of different bands and nations, he organized a synchronized attack on British forts in May 1763 that devastated the British.

Although the British issued a directive that land between the Appalachians and the Mississippi river was reserved as Native American hunting grounds, Native Americans continued to fight the British for control of the area. Governor-General Jeffrey Amherst didn't believe in fighting fair and suggested giving blankets infected with smallpox to the Native Americans. The British reportedly did just this at a 1764 peace conference in Pittsburgh. Chief Pontiac continued to fight against settlers and soldiers but eventually lost to the British and agreed to peace in 1766.

Native soldiers defeat General Braddock in the French and Indian War.

The American Revolution and Native Americans

NATIVE AMERICANS in the East were wary of the new peace that came with the British winning the French and Indian War. The British soon forgot the directive about hunting grounds as settlers moved into the Great Lakes region, which led to war with the Delaware and Shawnee who lived in the area. This angered the Six Nations Confederacy, who considered themselves to be the elder brothers to the Delaware and Shawnee. They questioned why the colonists weren't keeping their agreements to stay in the East.

Native Americans also noted an increasing division between the two groups of white people—the British military and the colonists. When the colonists were forced to pay for the French and Indian War through increased taxes, the colonists dressed as Native Americans to dump British tea into Boston Harbor. Soon, the American Revolution had begun, and once again, Native American nations were strongly encouraged to take sides. When the British warned against taking the side of the colonists, a Seneca warrior told them, "You want us to destroy ourselves in your War and they advise us to live in Peace. Their advice we intend to follow."

A Mohawk chief, Thayendanegea, better known as Joseph Brant, visited England in 1775–76 and spoke with King George III. Brant refused to bow to the king but offered to shake his hand. He also told King George, "Cease then to call yourselves Christians, lest you declare to the world your hypocrisy. Cease too to call other nations savage, when you are tenfold more the children of cruelty than they."

Born in 1742, Brant had attended Moor's Charity School for Indians in Connecticut as a boy. In addition to learning to speak English, Brant studied Western history and literature. After his sister married the British superintendent for northern Indian affairs, Brant followed his brother-in-law into the battles of the French and Indian War at the age of 13.

Instead of being offended by Brant's words to the king, the British seemed quite taken with him, and they honored him. This probably influenced Brant to support the British against the colonists, although several Native American nations threw their support behind the British in hopes that the colonists would leave America if the British won. Brant returned to the colonies and attempted to convince others within the Six Nations to support the British. Four of the six nations agreed, possibly influenced by the large amount of provisions the British gave to the Six Nations. The Oneida and the Tuscarora refused. The Six Nations were divided.

The American colonists concentrated on the nations to the south—the Cherokee, Choctaw, Creek, and Chickasaw—to persuade them to fight against the British. Yet these people had also had problems with colonists invading their land. The Creeks took the side of the British, and the Choctaw remained neutral. When a native delegation of Mohawk, Shawnee, and Delaware arrived, they were able to convince the Cherokee to join the British. Colonial soldiers responded by burning Cherokee homes, forcing the Cherokee farther west, and taking others as slaves. Battles continued in the South through 1781 until the Cherokee and Chickasaw negotiated peace with the colonists.

Thayendanegea, also known as Joseph Brant.

After the War

THE TREATY of Paris, signaling the end of the American Revolution, not only gave the new Americans the 13 colonies but also the territories in the Ohio Valley. As they created their new government, the first secretary of state, Thomas Jefferson, and President George Washington promised a policy of honor toward Native Americans in which "their land and property shall never be taken from them without their consent."

Chief Brant of the Mohawk couldn't get the Americans to agree to a land settlement, so he and a large group of Mohawk relocated to Canada in Brantford, Ontario. Brant continued to work for the Mohawk. He also wrote about the Mohawk leader who became an Onondaga chief, Hiawatha, and translated the Bible into the Mohawk language.

Farther west of the Appalachians, the hunting grounds and permanent homes of many native communities was called the Northwest Territory. Before the 19th century began, the federal government sold the land to new settlers. Eventually the Northwest Territory became five states: Ohio, Indiana, Illinois, Michigan, and Wisconsin.

South of the Northwest Territory, settlers began raiding native villages in Kentucky. The Miami and Shawnee people combined forces to

NATIVE AMERICAN SLAVERY

Seizing captive slaves from enemy Indian nations was an expected consequence of war among Native Americans before the arrival of Europeans. However, large-scale Native American slavery came with European exploration, particularly the British and the Spanish. Ponce de Leon, Hernando de Soto, and Coronado all forced slavery upon Native Americans. Later settlers used Native American slaves as forced labor on plantations in the southeastern United States and in the Caribbean West Indies.

Until 1720, tens of thousands of Native Americans were enslaved. Some were captives from Native American conflicts who were sold to the British. While some Native American slavery continued later into the century, the colonists began to prefer the African slaves being brought to America in mass numbers.

As Native Americans in the Southeast adopted more European customs, they began participating in the slave trade. Some Native Americans assisted African slaves in escaping, but many prosperous Cherokee, Choctaw, and Chickasaw owned African slaves in the late 18th and early 19th centuries. It's estimated that 15,000 African slaves also traveled the Trail of Tears to Indian Territory.

One nation that didn't enslave African Americans but lived, worked, and fought alongside them were the Seminole of Florida. Many escaped slaves joined the Seminole Nation. In Indian Territory, Seminole people defended African Americans from Cherokee and Muscogee nations. After the Civil War, hundreds of African Americans joined the Seminole Nation as Seminole Freedmen. Descendants of Freedmen-Seminole unions are tribal members.

fight back. Their goal was to keep these settlers north of the Ohio River. President Washington sent troops, but they were soundly defeated and lost more than 600 men. Eventually, the Americans defeated the Shawnee at Fallen Timbers (near Toledo, Ohio), and the Shawnee signed over Ohio. One Shawnee chief, Tecumseh, disagreed with the decision.

Tecumseh was born the fifth of nine children to a Shawnee warrior and a Muscogee (Creek) woman. After his father died in 1774 at the Battle of Point Pleasant, his mother moved west to Indiana. Eleven-year-old Tecumseh stayed in the Ohio Territory with his older brother and sister. His brother, Chiksika, trained Tecumseh to be a warrior. Tecumseh first tried out his new skills at age 14 in a conflict against the American soldiers. The battlefield sent him to a panic, and he fled. He was so humiliated by this experience that he became determined to be the best warrior he could be.

In 1782, after the Battle of Piqua, the Shawnee retreated to the Maumee River where they renewed their efforts against white settlement. Tecumseh became a formidable opponent for the white Americans. When Tecumseh was 23 years old, he led Shawnee warriors against the troops of Arthur St. Clair at Fort Recovery, Ohio. The U.S. Army suffered one of its worst defeats to date with the loss over 918 men. Tecumseh only had 61 casualties.

Tecumseh's skills as a warrior and leader were admired by many, but still he could not stop the white people from coming. Familiar with the greed of the American settler, Tecumseh continued to lead his people against settlers who wanted Shawnee land. He was also angered by Shawnee and other tribes who had signed over land to the settlers. The only way to win, Tecumseh decided, was for Native Americans to unite.

In the early 1800s, Tecumseh proposed forming a confederacy of Indian nations, similar to the Six Nations Confederacy but composed of tribes west of the Appalachian Mountains. He hoped the confederacy would keep native leaders from selling land that belonged to everyone. "Sell a country! Why not sell the air, the great sea, as well as the Earth? Did not the Great Spirit make them all for the use of his children?" he asked.

The death of Tecumseh.

Tecumseh's younger brother, Tenskwatawa, was known as the Prophet, particularly after he predicted an eclipse of the sun. The Prophet said that native people must give up white customs. He spread the message that if native people returned to their native ways, the Master of Life would remove the white people from their land. This prophecy helped Tecumseh unite native people as he became one of the first Native Americans to embrace Pan-Indian unity over tribal loyalty.

The Shawnee and other bands met at a village in Indiana Territory known as Prophetstown. While Tecumseh was away to recruit other Native American nations, American soldiers attacked Prophetstown and destroyed it. The loss led to a weakened confederacy, so Tecumseh supported the British in the War of 1812. The Shawnee warrior and leader died in the Battle of the Thames in 1813.

The Nations of the Southeast

Several Native American nations called the southeastern United States home, including the Cherokee, Choctaw, Chickasaw, and the Creek (Muscogee). They shared similar ways of adapting to a European lifestyle, such as permanent homes and farming. While some may have migrated from other parts of the United States, others, such as the Creek, may have

MARY MUSGROVE MATTHEWS BOSOMWORTH

Around 1700, a daughter was born to a Muscogee woman and an English trader named Edward Griffin. Known as Mary among the settlers, she was called Coosaponakeesa of the Wind Clan by the Muscogee. Growing up with a foot in each culture, Mary learned the languages and cultures of both English and Muscogee well.

In 1717, Mary married the English trader John Musgrove and helped him set up a trading post near the Savannah River. She began serving as an interpreter at this time, particularly for James Oglethorpe, who founded the Colony of Georgia in 1732. She was believed to be an important part of the peaceful founding of the colony and its first city, Savannah.

When her husband died in 1735, Mary Musgrove moved the trading post to Yamacraw Bluff, where it became an important trading post for the area. After marrying Jacob Matthews in 1737, she established another trading post at Mount Venture. After Matthews's death, she married her third husband, Reverend Thomas Bosomworth. This marriage increased her status in colonial society. Together, Mary and her husband traveled among Muscogee villages and interpreted for English leaders. Even with her power, she experienced trouble with the colonial government over land claims given to her by Muscogee chiefs. She pursued her claims for over 10 years, even traveling to England to plead her case. A compromise was eventually reached. She died on St. Catherines Island sometime after 1763.

Today, Coosaponakeesa, or Mary Musgrove Matthews Bosomworth, is best known for interpreting and working to maintain peace between the English and the Muscogee. She was inducted into Georgia Women of Achievement in 1993.

been descended from the prehistoric Mississippian Culture Etowah Mounds people who lived in the area until the early 1500s. The Etowah archeological site covers 52 acres with three large mounds and several smaller ones.

The southeastern Native Americans first had contact with European explorers. A trade relationship developed by exchanging furs for manufactured goods—guns and farming and cooking equipment. The Spanish had settlements in Florida, the British in Virginia, and the French in Louisiana. The growth of the fur trade caused animals to become scarcer, and many native people turned to farming. As in other parts of the United States, the people of the Southeast also suffered from exposure to European diseases such as smallpox.

When southeastern native groups supported the losing side during a European conflict, they were often punished through the taking of their land. Yet for the most part, the early U.S. government adopted a paternalistic attitude toward the native people of the South. The U.S. government often sent Indian agents to live among specific Native American nations to dispense supplies and keep an eye on things. It was just a matter of time before the white settlers began moving onto tribal lands and claiming them for their own.

Like many Native American groups, the Creek received the name they became known as from people outside their communities. Since some of the Creek lived near Ochese Creek, the British tradesmen shortened it to Creek. Actually these people shared the same Muskogean language and referred to themselves as Musco-gee. The Muscogee people established confederacies with other Muskogean towns and villages for protection against northern enemies.

The towns were laid out around a pascova, or plaza, where ceremonies, dancing, games, and festivals such as the Green Corn Festival were held. Plazas also included a rotunda for council meetings and an open-air summer council house. Smaller villages were aligned with a specific town, governed by a chief called a mico. When a village grew to 400 to 600 people, it would split and form a new nearby village.

By the beginning of the 18th century, Muscogee towns began to spread out with acres of crops for corn, rice, and potatoes. Many people raised livestock as well. Log homes starting replacing traditional huts with wood or grass roofs. Some Muscogee became quite successful by the time the Colony of Georgia was founded in 1732. In fact, the richest woman was the daughter of a English trader and a Muscogee woman. Mary Musgrove Matthews Bosomworth was a prosperous landowner with several trading posts and sometimes served as an interpreter for the British.

Sequoyah

THE CHEROKEE of North Carolina and Georgia also had towns and European-style homes, but they had something the other Native Americans didn't: a written language that allowed them to start a newspaper and create books. A written language also allowed the Cherokee to start writing some of their own history. All of this was possible because of one Cherokee—Sequoyah.

Sequoyah was a mixed-race Cherokee man born in 1776 in the Cherokee village of Tuskegee that overlooked the Tennessee and Tellico rivers. His father was a fur trader that he never knew. His mother was the daughter of a Cherokee chief. Sequoyah married a Cherokee woman and worked as a silversmith. He also worked as a blacksmith and a farmer and enjoyed sketching animals and people.

During the War of 1812, Sequoyah and other Cherokee men fought against the British under General Andrew Jackson. Although he could speak English, Sequoyah had never learned to write it. The Cherokee watched as the white American soldiers wrote to their families. When the war ended, Sequoyah decided to create a writing system for the Cherokee people.

It took time to create symbols to form words—12 years. Friends and family worried about his obsession. His wife even burned down his workshop to get him to stop, but he was committed to finding a way to communicate in Cherokee on paper.

Sequoyah created 85 symbols to represent sounds and taught them to his daughter, Ahyokeh. In 1821, Sequoyah introduced his Cherokee syllabary to the rest of his people by demonstrating it with his daughter. Within months, thousands of Cherokee were reading and writing. Four years later, the people had translated hymns and the Bible into Cherokee. Religious pamphlets, legal documents, and educational materials followed. By 1828, the first bilingual newspaper was created. The *Cherokee Phoenix* was a newspaper published in both Cherokee and English. In the same year, Sequoyah also left for Indian Territory with many of his people on the Trail of Tears (see page 60).

Sequoyah received a silver medal from the Cherokee for his contributions. He remained active in Cherokee affairs until his death in 1843. His birthplace is now covered by Tellico Reservoir, but nearby, the Sequoyah Birthplace Museum in Tennessee recognizes his achievements.

(ABOVE) Sequoyah.
(BELOW) A copy of the *Cherokee Phoenix*.

5

HEADING WEST

AFTER APPROXIMATELY 200 years of settlement in the eastern United States, white Americans were getting restless. Large numbers of immigrants were arriving daily from Europe, and all the states had seen increases in population. In just 40 years, the population of Georgia tripled twice.

In 1803, the United States purchased the Louisiana Territory from the French for $15 million dollars. The purchase greatly increased U.S. holdings of land west of the Mississippi. In fact, the United States doubled in territory size. The Louisiana Purchase included parts of 14 states, almost a quarter of the land area of the United States today. The Louisiana Purchase not only affected Native American nations living within its boundaries, but also was the beginning of opening up the West to white settlers.

The Bureau of Indian Affairs began taking a more aggressive stance toward the Native American population, particularly when set-tlers, who were ignoring land boundaries, complained about the native population. The Bureau of Indian Affairs oversaw the various agencies that dealt with Native Americans, from those who made the decisions in the nation's capitol down to individual Indian agents who worked directly with the tribes.

By 1828, only 125,000 Native Americans remained east of the Mississippi River. Almost half of that number lived in Georgia, Alabama, and Mississippi, where they owned millions of acres of land. But the white farmers and plantation owners saw the potential for growing

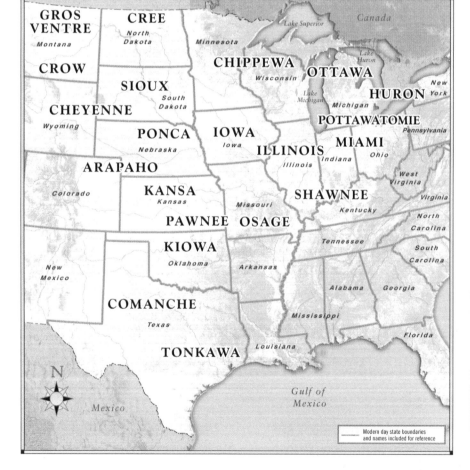

(ABOVE) The Louisiana Purchase.

cotton on that land. Then, when gold was discovered on Cherokee land in the North Georgia mountains, large numbers of squatters invaded that area. The Georgia state government's solution was to remove the Cherokee from Georgia entirely.

Indian Removal

THE STATE of Georgia and white settlers throughout the South found what they were looking for in the seventh president of the United States, Andrew Jackson. A self-taught attorney and politician from Tennessee, Jackson identified with the white settlers, even though he had adopted an orphaned Muscogee (Creek) boy 15 years before he assumed the office of the presidency. His troops most likely killed the boy's family during the Creek Wars.

When Jackson took office in 1829, he introduced the Indian Removal Act, which allowed southeastern tribes to exchange their land east of the Mississippi River for lands west of the Mississippi. While some Native Americans went peacefully, many resisted the relocation policy because they did not want to leave their homes. Indian Removal was also opposed by other Americans, including leading statesman and speaker Daniel Webster and frontiersman and congressman Davy Crockett. Regardless, Congress passed the Indian Removal bill in 1830. Disgusted by politics that forced people off their land, Crockett left political office and headed to Texas, where he joined the fight at the Alamo.

THE BUREAU OF INDIAN AFFAIRS

In the early years of U.S. history, commissioners from the War Department were appointed for Indian Affairs. Their main duty was to negotiate treaties between the U.S. government and various nations. Early commissioners included Benjamin Franklin and Patrick Henry.

Secretary of War John C. Calhoun established the Bureau of Indian Affairs (BIA) in 1824 as an office within the War Department. It was often called the Office of Indian Affairs. In the beginning, the BIA was led by military men, but Congress transferred control to the new Department of the Interior in 1849.

During Indian Removal, the BIA's role centered on getting food and supplies to Native American nations that had treaties with the government. Yet the BIA was only as good as the agents who dealt directly with Native Americans, and many were dishonest. In 1868, President Grant attempted to reorganize the Office of Indian Affairs by appointing missionaries and Quakers as Indian agents, instead of political appointees. A year later, Grant appointed the first Native American—a Seneca—to head the organization: Brigadier General Ely Parker (Donehogawa).

When the government focused on placing many Native Americans in the West on reservations, the BIA continued to distribute supplies but also operated schools and oversaw tribal operations. As laws passed that allowed Native American nations to govern themselves, the BIA's role shifted to an advisory role.

Today, the BIA is the oldest department within the Department of the Interior. Before the 1930s, most BIA employees were nonnative. Today, approximately 95 percent are Native Americans who provide services to approximately 1.7 million Native Americans and Alaskan Natives. Duties include managing 66 million acres of land held in trust for these populations.

Five nations were most affected by this bill: Cherokee, Choctaw, Chickasaw, Muscogee (Creek), and Seminole. These nations had assimilated to life among the white Americans. They wore European clothing and adopted many of the European customs. They built homes, schools, churches, and roads. They had governments in which elected officials represented the larger population. These nations became known as the Five Civilized Tribes due to their knowledge and use of Euro-American items and customs.

The Trail of Tears

MISSISSIPPI BECAME the first state to start removal of the tribes. Although they didn't speak for the entire Choctaw Nation, some Choctaw leaders signed the Treaty of Dancing Rabbit Creek, ceding all lands east of the Mississippi River in exchange for land in Indian Territory, which would later make up most of the State of Oklahoma. Between 1831 and 1833, large numbers of the Choctaw Nation were forced out of Mississippi by this treaty. Removal was disorganized, and many people died of starvation, exposure, and a cholera epidemic.

Alabama and Georgia soon followed, forcing the Muscogee from their homes. Numerous conflicts with settlers and the government had left many Muscogee impoverished, which made the journey to Indian Territory even more difficult. People often had to leave for Indian Territory with only what they could carry. Those who resisted had to march bound in chains. The journey was over 800 miles by land, and most people were walking with inadequate clothing for winter travel. Most traveled barefoot, and

Davy Crockett, who left Congress in protest of the Indian Removal Act.

any shoes were soon falling to pieces. Many couldn't keep walking on frostbitten feet and were exhausted. They were left by the side of the road. The 400 miles by water wasn't much better, as officials crowded as many Native Americans as possible onto barges. During one trip up the Mississippi River, a steamboat collided with a boat crowded with Muscogee people. The boat was cut in half, killing 311 Muscogee people.

Approximately 3,500 people died during the forced migration to Indian Territory.

The government also asked Muscogee leaders to help with the capture of Seminoles in northern Florida. In return, the Muscogee would be in charge of the shared land in Indian Territory. Obviously, it was an agreement that left many Seminole angry. Although some had already made the journey to Indian Territory, others refused, which led to the Second Seminole War.

It took seven years to forcibly remove most of the Seminole people to Indian Territory. Some Seminole hid from soldiers, who continued to round up Seminole people for forced migration. General Zachary Taylor and his forces pursued escaped Seminole prisoners into late 1838. In December of that year, hundreds of Seminole warriors waited at Lake Okeechobee in central Florida for General Zachary Taylor and his forces of over a thousand who were pursuing escaped Seminoles. The Seminole defeated

OSCEOLA

In 1835, President Jackson sent a letter to the Seminole informing them that they must sign a treaty giving up their lands. A Seminole warrior named Osceola reportedly stabbed the treaty with his knife. Afterward, he continued to lead the Seminole in resistance against the United States and the removal policies by orchestrating several successful battles.

Osceola was not a chief but he was a skilled speaker and greatly influenced the Seminole with his words and his bravery. The Seminole built their villages deep in the swamps to avoid capture. In 1836, many people in Florida, Seminole and settlers alike, became ill with malaria. The following year, General Thomas Jessup arrived with 5,000 troops. With a weakened Seminole people and also sick with malaria, Osceola surrendered under a white flag of truce. Jessup's troops threw down the white flag and put Osceola in chains. In anger over this betrayal, the Seminole continued to fight. Meanwhile, Osceola was placed in a prison cell in Charleston, South Carolina, where he died on January 30, 1838.

the army at the Battle of Okeechobee. When it ended on Christmas Day, the U.S. Army had lost 28 soldiers and had 112 wounded. Only 10 Seminoles died in the battle.

When the Second Seminole War end in 1842, the U.S. Army had lost 1,500 men and over $20 million had been spent. The United States continued to pursue the Seminole in Florida. Those who were caught were rounded up like livestock along with several hundred former African slaves and forced to Indian Territory. Others remained hidden in Florida until the U.S. government ceased to hunt them. The

Seminole people can proudly attest to never signing a peace treaty with the United States. Today, the Seminole have significant tribes in both Florida and Oklahoma.

Although the Treaty of Pontotoc Creek ceding Chickasaw land in Mississippi was ratified in early 1833, it would take four more years before the Chickasaw made the trip to Indian Territory. Yet even before that, white squatters began settling on Chickasaw land that bordered upon Mississippi and Alabama, and the government would not stop them. When the Chickasaw people arrived in Indian Territory, they settled on the western parcels of land belonging to the Choctaw. The Cherokee and Choctaw had the largest divisions of Indian Territory bordering Arkansas, with the Cherokee to the north and the Choctaw in the south. The Muscogee and Seminole occupied sections in central Indian Territory.

The Cherokee decided to fight against Indian Removal in court. Specifically, they declared that if they were an independent nation, they shouldn't be subject to state or federal laws. By 1832, the Supreme Court agreed that the Cherokee were indeed a sovereign nation not subject to the Indian Removal Act. Instead, removal would have to be done by treaty.

U.S. commissioners met with a small group of Cherokee in 1835. This group, which included Major Ridge, John Ridge, and Elias Boudinot (editor of the Cherokee newspaper, the *Cherokee Phoenix*), signed the New Echota Treaty, ceding all Cherokee land east of the Mississippi to the government for $5 million. Many Cherokee cried in outrage that a few people were allowed to speak and make decisions for the entire nation.

Cherokee Chief John Ross made many trips to Washington, D.C., to try to convince U.S. officials of the rights of the Cherokee to remain on their lands. When Ross returned home from the capitol in 1835, he found white settlers living in his house. While he had been negotiating with the federal government, the Georgia government held a land lottery and gave his home to someone else.

Cherokee removal began in 1838. The first general in charge of Cherokee removal, John Wool, resigned in protest. General Winfield Scott was hired to supervise the removal with the help of 7,000 soldiers. They began by removing Cherokee people from their homes at gunpoint and locking them up in stockades. The people weren't even allowed to gather their belongings. Many families were separated. Three groups left that summer for the six-month trip. Crowding, disease, and drinking unsanitary water led to many deaths. In one group, three to five people a day died. One quarter of the people—4,000—died because of the unsanitary conditions. The children and

Cherokee Chief John Ross.

the elderly were the first to die on the thousand-mile walk that provided little in the way of food or resources.

Reverend Daniel Sabine Butrick had been a missionary to the Cherokee for approximately 20 years when Cherokee Removal began. A close friend of Chief John Ross, Butrick traveled with the third group of approximately 1,070 people who left for Indian Territory in the summer of 1838. He kept a journal of the journey.

Monday (June 11 or 18, 1838) — The weather being extremely warm and dry, many of the Cherokees are sick especially at Calhoon where, we understand, from four to ten die in a day.

One returning from the camps was overtaken by a gentleman who had been with a boat load of dear Cherokee prisoners. Of the second boat load he says thirty had died when he met them at Waterloo, and great sickness was prevailing.

Chief Ross, who lost his own wife on the Trail of Tears, convinced General Scott to allow the Cherokee to take over the removal from the army soldiers. in July 1838. At a council meeting, Ross and six others were elected as the Emigration Management Committee to oversee the arrangements. Ross negotiated a contract that allowed for $65.88 per person for

the trip. This provided $0.16 a day for food and $0.40 a day per horse or ox. By November, the remaining Cherokee were divided into smaller groups to take various routes to Indian Territory. They foraged for food to supplement their limited rations. Muddy roads and ice-covered rivers made travel hazardous, but fewer Cherokee died when they took charge of their own move.

The Trail of Tears exhibit at the Cherokee Heritage Center.

Rebecca Neugin was three years old at the time of removal. She recalled her mother being allowed to go back to their home for bedding and grabbing as many cooking utensils as she could, which helped her family survive, Neugin explained to historian Grant Foreman.

The people got so tired of eating salt pork on the journey that my father would walk through the woods as we traveled, hunting for turkeys and deer which he brought into camp to feed us. Camp was usually made at some place where water was to be had and when we stopped and prepared to cook our food other emigrants who had been driven from their homes without opportunity to secure cooking utensils came to our camp to use our pots and kettles. There was much sickness among the emigrants and a great many little children died of whooping cough.

A small group of Cherokee escaped into the North Carolina mountains. Today, they are known as the Eastern Band of Cherokees. With tempers high after the disastrous Trail of Tears, groups within the Ross party planned the execution of the Cherokee men who had signed the Treaty of New Echota. It is not known if Principal Chief John Ross supported this decision or tried to stop it. John Rollin Ridge was 12 years old when he saw his father, John Ridge, and grandfather, Major Ridge, executed. John Rollin Ridge later became the first Native American novelist when his book, *The Life and Adventures of Joaquin Murieta, the Celebrated California Bandit* (1854), was published.

Like the Eastern Band of Cherokee, some Choctaw and Seminole people remained behind and today have bands living in Mississippi and Florida respectively. Yet the majority of each nation made the dangerous trek with a large, unnecessary loss of life. Although the term "Trail of Tears" was first associated with the Cherokee people, it applied to all five of the southeastern U.S. nations forced from their homes only to lose children, spouses, and grandparents.

Westward Expansion

AFTER THE explorations of Lewis and Clark in the early 1800s, Euro-Americans started looking to the West as the place for freedom and adventure. Yet just as the East Coast had already been populated by people, so was the West. Hundreds of nations lived west of the Mississippi. Many were Plains people such as the Sioux, Apache, Comanche, and Arapaho. These nomadic bands moved from place to place as they followed food sources like the bison. Other nations, such as the Pueblo people, stayed in one place and farmed. The Pawnee did both.

Pawnee villages sat alongside rivers throughout Nebraska. People lived in earth lodges measuring about 40 feet around. Fields of corn, squash, beans, and pumpkins surrounded the villages. After the plants were established, the Pawnee often left for a summer buffalo hunt. When they returned in early autumn, they harvested their crops. If there was time, they might undertake one more buffalo hunt to store food for winter. The Pawnee were great hunters.

Pawnee men were often easy to identify in the 1800s. Many added paint and buffalo fat to their hair, which made it look like a horn. The Pawnee became known for being good scouts who occasionally helped the U.S. army, particularly against enemy nations such as the Lakota.

Native American nations that followed the buffalo usually lived in tepees, which were easy to move from place to place. Before the arrival of the Spanish to the Southwest, dogs carried belongings from place to place on a framework of poles called a travois that was attached to the dogs by leather straps. By the time explorers and settlers from the East arrived, the Plains people were accomplished horsemen who used horses to drag the poles used for the tepee frames. The remainder of their belongings sat on the poles.

Plains people were determined to continue living on the plains as they had been doing for

Make Jerky

PLAINS TRIBES were often nomadic, moving from place to place as they followed the buffalo. They weren't able to carry much extra equipment or food. Many native people carried jerky—dried meat strips—as a quick and easy food while traveling. Jerky was often made from buffalo or elk, but you can make your own jerky with lean beef.

Adult supervision required

Materials

◆ Lean cut of beef, such as sirloin

◆ Knife

◆ Vinegar

◆ Coarse salt (kosher or sea salt)

◆ Flavorings (such as soy sauce, Worcestershire sauce, garlic powder, or teriyaki sauce)

◆ Nonstick cooking spray, such as Pam

◆ Aluminum foil

Remove all visible fat from a piece of lean beef—fat causes jerky to spoil fast. Cut remaining beef into thin strips.

Make a marinade of vinegar and salt using approximately ½ cup of vinegar and 1 teaspoon of salt per pound of meat. Place the strips of meat into a marinade and refrigerate for 4 to 24 hours. After at least four hours in the marinade, remove the meat from the marinade and season as you want. Some people add hot sauce for a spicy jerky.

Spray the racks in your oven with a nonstick cooking spray. Set the oven to 150°F and lay the strips of meat over the racks. Mold a piece of aluminum foil into a pan. Place it on the rack below the jerky to catch any drippings. The temperature isn't as high as for normal cooking because you are drying the meat, not cooking it. Keep meat in the low heat until the jerky is deep brown and shriveled. It will take from 6 to 12 hours. Cut one strip to check that jerky is done inside, too. Store in sealed plastic bags.

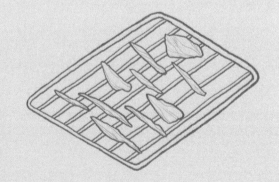

many hundreds of years. The U.S. military established forts to protect the settlers in the West. Keeping settlers safe became a challenge when 50,000 gold-hungry people traveled through Lakota country headed for California's gold fields.

Trading posts and Indian agencies also populated the plains. The first treaties involved exchanging food and goods to ensure safe passage for settlers. Later, the treaties concentrated on land ownership. In particular, the years from 1853 to 1856 involved 52 treaties concerning 174 million acres of land. Eventually, every single treaty had been broken—each by the U.S. government.

A buffalo hunt.

The Civil War

THE FEDERAL government took time out from conquering the West, between 1861 to 1865, for the Civil War. The division between families and neighbors didn't just affect Euro-Americans, it also affected Native Americans, who were once again asked to pick sides.

The South created its own Bureau of Indian Affairs that promised the return of tribal lands in exchange for joining the Confederacy in its fight against the North. Most of the Choctaw and Chickasaw people joined the Confederacy. The other nations were divided, with some supporting the North and others the South. Within the Cherokee Nation, in particular, there was much fighting about which side to support.

Regiments of Native American soldiers found themselves fighting alongside or against white and African American regiments. Many Native Americans were accomplished soldiers and leaders. A good example was Cherokee General Stand Watie.

Stand Watie was born in New Echota in the Cherokee Nation. He took his name from combining his Cherokee and Christian names. He and several family members (Elias Boudinot, Major Ridge, and John Ridge) were part of a group who advocated Cherokee removal to Indian Territory. Although they weren't authorized to, Watie and his relatives signed the New Echota Treaty, which committed the Cherokee to removal. Watie immigrated to Indian Territory in 1837 and settled in the northeastern part of the new Cherokee Nation. While those who signed the New Echota Treaty were sentenced to death, Watie went into hiding for a few years after being warned of the executions. He remained the leader of the party or faction opposing John Ross, sometimes referred to as the Ridge-Watie party, until 1846 when Ross and Watie made peace.

When the Civil War began, Watie joined the Confederacy as a colonel of the First Regiment of Cherokee Mounted Volunteers. Also in 1862, Watie became principal chief of the Cherokee. Watie's regiment had many victories, and he was promoted to brigadier general in May 1864. In the last days of the war, he was appointed commander of the Indian Division of Indian Territory. General Stand Watie was the last Confederate general to surrender to the Union in 1865.

After the war ended in victory for the North, the five nations in Indian Territory were punished for providing assistance to the Confederacy. The western half of Indian Territory was taken from them and given to the more than 20 Native American nations that were coming to Indian Territory.

THE WILD BUFFALO ARE NO MORE

About 20,000 years ago, many millions of bison, better known as American buffalo, populated the Great Plains. Although they weighed up to a ton, these huge, shaggy beasts could run up to 35 miles an hour for a long distance. This made them difficult to hunt. Early people used techniques such as buffalo jumps, where they herded buffalo in a stampede off a cliff. When horses came to the Plains people, riders raced alongside buffalo and brought them down with arrows, spears, or bullets.

Native Americans wasted nothing. They killed only as only much as they could eat or carry with them, and every part of the buffalo was used. The hides kept them warm, and the bones made effective tools. Because native people never killed more than they needed, there were always enough buffalo.

A buffalo today.

When the white settlers arrived on the plains, they found that they could sell buffalo hides for a lot of money. Soon the plains were littered with the rotting bodies of buffalo as settlers took only the hides and left the meat. In the winter of 1872, more than 1.5 million buffalo hides were shipped back east. By 1880, the buffalo had almost disappeared. Their demise coincided with the large number of Native American bands entering reservations.

From a low of approximately 1,000 buffalo in the 1880s, conservation efforts have increased numbers to approximately half a million today. Most are privately owned, although 30,000 are part of conservation herds in national parks and wildlife refuges.

The Indian Wars

ALTHOUGH THE U.S. Army was consumed with the Civil War, they didn't neglect the plains. The Plains tribes had negotiated previous agreements to give American settlers safe passage through Indian lands. But the plan changed to one of placing Plains tribes in Indian Territory or on reservations instead. The Oto, Missouri, Ponca, and Pawnee were some of the many nations relocated to Indian Territory. Other nations fought long and hard against being confined to a specific piece of land. Battles became common.

Perhaps one of the most tragic events was the Sand Creek Massacre of 1864. As dawn broke on the chilly morning of November 29, a village of Cheyenne and Arapaho people found themselves under attack from volunteers of the First and Third Colorado Regiments.

George Bent, the son of a Cheyenne woman and a white pioneer, was still in bed when he heard that soldiers were coming. He looked out of his lodge to see one group of soldiers coming from the east and another from the west.

About 53 men were killed and 110 women and children killed, 163 in all killed. Lots of men, women, and children were wounded.... The village was on north side of Sand Creek, about 146 lodges of Cheyennes.... Women and children ran up bed of Sand Creek about 2½ miles and dug pits under bank in sand.

Conflicts and wars continued as the government tried to force Native Americans onto reservations. The Southern Plains War of 1868–69 pitted the forces of General Sheridan against the Comanche, Cheyenne, Arapaho, Kiowa, and Lakota. Seventy-two Kiowa, Cheyenne, and Arapaho warriors were taken prisoner and transported to Fort Marion in St. Augustine, Florida.

The Native American nations split up after the Southern Plains War. The U.S. army pursued them all, forcing them to reservation life.

"I Will Fight No More Forever."

ONE OF the most famous leaders of the Nez Percé nation in the Pacific Northwest was Chief Joseph. Born in Oregon in 1840, he was named Hin-mah-too-yah-lat-kekt, or Thunder Rolling Down the Mountain. When Chief Joseph was a boy, his father converted to Christianity and took the name of Joseph. The father became Joseph the Elder and his son, Joseph the Younger.

Joseph the Elder was a major advocate of peace with the Americans and helped establish a Nez Percé reservation. But in 1863 gold was discovered on Nez Percé land, and the government took back almost six million acres and wanted the tribe restricted to a small piece of land in Idaho. Joseph the Elder refused to sign a treaty or move his band. When he died in 1871, his son succeeded him.

Chief Joseph.

QUANAH PARKER

Quanah Parker was born the son of a Comanche chief, Peta Nocona, and a white captive, Cynthia Ann Parker. When he was still a young boy, his mother and sister were recaptured by soldiers. It's been said that they couldn't readjust to living in white culture, and both died within a few years.

At a young age, Quanah distinguished himself as a warrior and became a leader of the Kwahadi Comanche. As the last Comanche war chief, he reportedly never lost a battle. Although the Kwahadi Comanche were the last band to remain free, they were weary of running and decided to surrender in 1875. Quanah Parker settled in southwest Oklahoma near Fort Sill, where he became a prosperous farmer, businessman, and one of the richest and most famous Native Americans of his day. Along with Geronimo, Parker rode in Theodore Roosevelt's 1905 inaugural parade. As successful as he was in the white world, he never forgot his native heritage and did much for the Comanche by serving as a judge and helping others prosper by leasing surplus land to white cattlemen. When he died in 1911, his funeral procession was over two miles long.

Quanah Parker.

Chief Joseph did everything he could to resist moving his band onto the reservation without going to war. In 1877, the army threatened to attack the Nez Percé unless they moved to the reservation. As Chief Joseph led his people to Idaho, a group of young, angry warriors began attacking white settlements. Although Chief Joseph had not ordered the attacks, he sided with the group that chose war over the reservation.

For three months, the Nez Percé band of 700, with less than 200 warriors, fought off 2,000 U.S. soldiers using military tactics that even impressed General William Tecumseh Sherman. Chief Joseph, like his father, had always advocated peace. He wasn't the war chief, but he proved to be a great leader for his people and one of the most eloquent speakers of the time. In his surrender speech, he said, "My heart is sick and sad. From where the sun now stands I will fight no more forever."

Sitting Bull

THE SURRENDER of important leaders such as Chief Joseph and Quanah Parker was publicized throughout the United States. However, two leaders remained elusive: Sitting Bull of the Hunkpapa Lakota and Geronimo of the Chiricahua Apache.

Sitting Bull, also known as Tatanka-Iyotanka, was a legendary chief and holy man whose courage inspired his people. Once, during a battle, he led four warriors out to the middle of a battleground. As they sat and shared a pipe, bullets whizzed by them. Yet they remained unharmed.

Sitting Bull is best known for his role in the Battle of Little Big Horn. When gold was discovered in the Black Hills in 1874, the white people decided to forget all about the Fort Laramie Treaty of 1868, which stated that this was Lakota land. When the Lakota refused to part with the land to which they felt a spiritual connection, Congress passed a law stating that no more treaties would be made with the Native American people. Furthermore, the government stated that all Lakota not residing on a reservation by 1876 would be treated as hostile.

As the army prepared for attack in the summer of 1876, Sitting Bull called upon the Lakota, Cheyenne, and Arapaho to fight together against the soldiers. While participating in the Sun Dance ritual, Sitting Bull had a vision of soldiers falling "like grasshoppers falling from the sky."

After the Oglala Lakota, led by Crazy Horse, defeated General Crook's troops, the Lakota moved their camp to Little Bighorn River. Word of Sitting Bull had spread as the Lakota were joined by 3,000 more Native Americans who

Sitting Bull.

Create a Totem Pole

WHEN EARLY missionaries arrived in the Pacific Northwest, they believed that the carved and painted poles reaching for the sky symbolized gods that the native people of the region worshipped. The missionaries were wrong. Instead, totem poles told the village who lived in the home behind the totem pole, usually a powerful or well-off family or clan. Totem poles more or less served as address markers.

Carved from single cedar trees up to 40 feet high, each totem pole was unique with carved animal figures that showed a clan history and privileges. It was a time-consuming task to cut, paint, and prepare a log. Like many other Native American artifacts, many totem poles were removed from their rightful places by museums and souvenir seekers. Since the passage of the Native American Graves Protection and Repatriation Act in 1990, some of them have been returned to their homes.

Materials
- ❖ Paper
- ❖ Drawing tools
- ❖ Clip art
- ❖ Glue stick
- ❖ Empty paper towel roll

Think about your family history. Remember some of the stories you've been told by family members. Ask older family members for information as well. Choose five or six things about your family that you want to represent. Pick symbols to represent those things. For example, if your family lives or originated from near the ocean, you may want to include a dolphin or whale.

Draw the symbols or find clip art to represent them. Cut, color, or paint these images. Glue the images on an empty paper towel roll, stacking one symbol on top of another.

Totem pole.

Arapaho Fry Bread

BREAD IS part of many traditional Native American meals. Some people made bread from ground-up corn, while others used meal made from acorns. The Zuni made a steamed bread, and fry bread was popular among many nations, particularly the Navajo. Fry bread is still a popular addition to meals or for special occasions. Not only does it serve as a base for Indian tacos, but it's also tasty all by itself when warm or served with honey. Try this Arapaho version of fry bread.

Adult supervision required

Materials
◆ ½ cup dry milk
◆ ⅓ cup baking powder
◆ 2 cups flour
◆ ¼ to ½ teaspoon salt
◆ 3½ cups water
◆ Vegetable oil for frying
◆ Deep frying skillet
◆ Metal tongs or something to turn bread while frying

Mix the dry milk, baking power, flour, and salt. Add the water to make dough. Knead the dough with your hands. You can cover them in flour to keep the dough from sticking too much.

Fill a skillet with oil about 1½ inches deep. Sprinkle some salt in the oil to keep the oil from burning or splattering too much. While the oil is heating over medium-high heat, pull off pieces of dough and make balls, each about the size of a golf ball. Flatten the balls slightly, and add them to the hot oil. Turn them over when they are brown on the bottom. Drain them on paper towels, and keep them warm until you're ready to eat.

had left their reservations. While at Little Bighorn, they were attacked by the Seventh Cavalry, led by General George Custer. Custer and his men suffered total defeat.

While the defeat was impressive, it only brought more soldiers to the area, all intent on capturing Sitting Bull. The leader moved his people into Canada for a time, but with the buffalo virtually gone from the plains, Sitting Bull had a difficult time feeding his people. He eventually surrendered in 1881 at Fort Buford in Montana. Sitting Bull was the last Lakota chief to surrender.

The Capture of Geronimo

GOYATHLAY, A Bedonkohe Apache, was born in New Mexico in 1829. Although not a chief, he became a spiritual leader of his wife's band, the Chiricahua Apache. Mexican soldiers gave this brave fighter another name, Geronimo, for the many raids he initiated against Mexico. In 1858 Geronimo returned home from a trading trip to find his wife and three children murdered by troops from Mexico. After this, Geronimo terrorized Mexican settlements. He became known as a fierce warrior, and stories of his supernatural abilities, such as being able to avoid bullets, spread throughout the territory.

The Chiricahua Apache were forcibly removed to an Arizona reservation in 1876, but Geronimo and his followers fled into Mexico. They were later arrested and returned to the reservation, but not for long. Geronimo said, "I was born on the prairies where the wind blew free and there was nothing to break the light of the sun. I was born where there were no enclosures."

After repeated escapes and surrenders, Geronimo surrendered a final time on September 4, 1886. He was originally confined at Forts Marion and Pickens in Florida but was later moved to Fort Sill in Oklahoma in 1894 where he lived the remainder of his days. Although Geronimo had a cell at Fort Sill, he didn't spend much time there. Geronimo became a rancher and made public appearances at events like the Louisiana Purchase Exposition and Theodore Roosevelt's inauguration. He died in 1909 and is buried in the Apache cemetery near Fort Sill.

Geronimo.

6

DESTRUCTION of a WAY of LIFE

As THE 1800s came to a close, Native Americans throughout the West, as well as the East, lived on reservations. Often, reservations were located on worthless land where farming and raising livestock was difficult. Supplies were scarce, or sometimes nonexistent. Hunting, long an important way to gather food, was no longer permitted on the reservations. While most nationalities had grown in population over 300 years in the United States, Native Americans weren't one of them. Sixty million native people had dwindled to 1 million.

The End of Indian Territory

THE MORE land white America accumulated, the more the government attempted to control Native Americans. In 1887, Congress passed the General Allotment Act, also known as the Dawes Act after the law's author, Senator Henry Dawes. The Dawes Act broke up lands held communally by various native nations and divided them into 160-acre allotments. Each head of a family received one-fourth of a section. Other single adults over 18 and orphaned children under 18 received one-eighth of a section. Other children under 18 received one-sixteenth of a section.

The original act exempted Indian Territory in addition to the Seneca (New York) and Lakota Sioux (Nebraska) reservations. Five years later the government changed the law to include all land belonging to Native Americans. Land in Indian Territory not claimed under the Dawes Act was considered surplus and renamed Oklahoma Territory. It was then opened up to homesteaders by "runs." Over 50,000 people moved into Oklahoma Territory on the first land run on April 22, 1889. When the gun fired at noon, people ran to the land they wanted and staked a claim. Three more land runs were held during the next six years until the government then decided it was easier to award land through lotteries or auctions.

Native Americans lost two-thirds of the land owned by treaty, and Indian Territory shrank dramatically. By 1907, Indian Territory was completely swallowed up and replaced with the 46th state—Oklahoma.

In 1903, a Kiowa man named Lone Wolf took his case against allotment to the Supreme Court. The Court ruled against him, stating that Congress had the power to break treaties. The Supreme Court also referred to the need for "Christian people" to govern "an ignorant and dependent race." This racist attitude was prevalent throughout the government in the early 20th century, and it was a contributing factor to why Native Americans were not given U.S. citizenship until 1924.

The Massacre of Wounded Knee

RESERVATION LIFE left many bands discouraged, particularly Plains people who were used to roaming free. Word began to spread of a Paiute shaman in Nevada who had a message of hope. His name was Wovoka, but people also referred to him as a messiah. Wovoka had a vision of a day when native people could live the old ways again with plentiful game: "A tidal wave of new soil would cover the Earth, bury the whites, and restore the prairie."

ROLL NUMBERS

The Dawes Act resulted in the use of roll numbers in many Native American communities. Each Native American had to register on a tribal roll and receive a roll number. Originally used in determining land allotment, roll numbers were later used by the BIA and tribal governments to determine citizenship in a Native American nation. The tribal roll number of an ancestor is needed to apply for a Certificate of Degree of Indian Blood, or CDIB, also known as a white card. The CDIB proves Native American heritage, allowing for tribal membership.

In order to bring this event about, he said, native people were to dance the Ghost Dance wearing special Ghost Shirts of white muslin decorated with feathers, symbols, or an eagle. Many Lakota also believed the Ghost Shirts would keep them safe from bullets. While many Plains nations practiced the Ghost Dance, it became especially important among the Lakota, who had lost so much.

By 1890, half of the land originally given to the Lakota had been taken back and sold to settlers. The land that was lost was the best hunting land, and some Lakota protested. The government responded by cutting off rations. With starvation and a cold winter approaching, the Lakota embraced the Ghost Dance as their last hope.

A panicked Indian Agent notified officials in Washington, D.C., about the "wild and crazy" Native Americans. President Benjamin Harrison ordered all unauthorized activities stopped. The secretary of war sent orders to stop the Ghost Dancing and arrest Chief Sitting Bull and Chief Big Foot of the Teton Sioux at the Standing Rock Reservation in the Dakotas. As he was being arrested by Indian Police (men of the tribe appointed as police officers by the Indian agent) under the orders of the agent at Standing Rock, Chief Sitting Bull was accidently shot and killed during a scuffle.

Although sick with pneumonia, Chief Big Foot moved his people to the Pine Ridge Res-

ervation, hoping for protection from Chief Red Cloud's band. The Seventh Cavalry of the U.S. Army intercepted them at Wounded Knee Creek in South Dakota. While Big Foot and his warriors talked with army officers, they heard shots fired. Soldiers and warriors grabbed for guns, and a storm of bullets rained down upon the camp. The soldiers perched on a hill above the camp, with Hotchkiss guns that worked

GHOST DANCE

With poverty and disease constant companions in the late 1880s, native people grasped for hope that their situation would improve. The Ghost Dance gave them something to believe in. More than a dance, the Ghost Dance was a religion that preached that traditional living would lead to a world reborn without white people.

The Ghost Dance.

Although meditation and prayer were important, there was also a ritual dance. After purification in a sweat lodge, dancers dressed in special Ghost Dance shirts and painted themselves with red paint. Dancers sang special songs while circling counterclockwise around a sacred tree. The tempo of the songs and dance increased as the Ghost Dance continued, sometimes for days. Participants sometimes fell to the ground as if dead and experienced visions of seeing beloved family members who had died.

like machine guns, spraying waves of bullets throughout the camp. Women and children ran through the clouds of smoke for a nearby ravine, but most didn't make it. When the shooting stopped, about 300 Lakota men, women, and children lay dead, as well as 25 soldiers. A blizzard blew through the camp, delaying body retrieval for a couple of days. The frozen bodies were buried in a long trench. Ghost Shirts were ripped from the bodies as souvenirs.

On December 29, 1890, the Indian Wars and the Ghost Dance movement officially ended at Wounded Knee.

Boarding Schools Divide Families

PRESIDENT HARRISON's administration focused Indian policy on encouraging assimilation, or integration, into white culture. This method meant taking away everything "Indian" about a person. Efforts at assimilating adults had limited success, so it was decided to start earlier by placing native children at Indian boarding schools.

Richard Pratt created the first of these schools, Carlisle Indian School, in Pennsylvania in 1879. Pratt's philosophy was "Kill the Indian, save the man." While the approximately 100 Indian boarding schools that sprang up from Pennsylvania to Washington to Oklahoma operated differently, they shared many similarities.

Admission to an Indian school wasn't voluntary. Children were taken from their homes, against family wishes, to faraway schools. While mothers, fathers, and grandparents stood by with tears in their eyes and their hands figuratively tied, children as young as five years old were pulled from clinging to their mothers' skirts and forced onto trains and wagons.

Native American actor and activist Floyd Red Crow Westerman remembered, even more than 60 years later, the trauma of leaving for boarding school. He had thought his mother

Big Foot's band.

didn't want him anymore until he saw that she was crying. Westerman then looked at the other families of children leaving for boarding school. "I'll never forget. All the mothers were crying."

One of the first things children faced when they arrived at school was the removal of their hair. Boys' hair was cut short. Girls' hair was cut or braided. Lakota children believed that hair was only cut when someone died. They found these haircuts very traumatic.

The children's hair was washed with kerosene to kill possible lice and their bodies were scrubbed with a harsh substance called lye. Students received new names and clothing. Discipline was strict. One of the first rules children learned was that they couldn't practice any of their customs or speak their own language. According to one student, "If we were caught speaking our language, we were punished severe. We might get a kerosene shampoo or a bar of yellow soap shoved in our mouth. That was just part of it." Students could only speak English or they might be spanked, sometimes in front of others as a lesson.

Indian boarding schools were a particular threat to Native American history. Previously, history was largely shared and communicated orally. Many nations that originated in the Southeast had tribal historians who were

(LEFT) A classroom at Carlisle School.
(BELOW) Digging potatoes at Carlisle School.

JIM THORPE

His name was Wa-Tho-Huck, meaning "Bright Path," and he is known as one of the greatest athletes the world has ever seen. Born in Prague, Oklahoma, in 1887, Thorpe was Pottawatomie, Sauk, and Fox. As a teen, he attended Carlisle Industrial Indian School where he ran track and played football, winning first team All-American in football for two years.

At the age of 24, Thorpe represented the U.S. track team at the 1912 Olympics in Belgium. He not only won gold medals for the pentathlon and the decathlon, he set records that took many years for anyone to beat. When awarding Thorpe his medals, King Gustav V exclaimed, "Sir, you are the greatest athlete in the world." Unfortunately, Thorpe was stripped of his medals in

Jim Thorpe playing baseball for the New York Giants.

1913 when it was discovered that he had played two semiprofessional seasons of baseball.

After the Olympics, Thorpe played baseball for six years, starting with the New York Giants. Always fascinated with football, he switched to playing that sport for another six years before he organized an all-Native team, the Oorang Indians. Thorpe created the American Professional Football Association, which evolved into the NFL (National Football League). He served as its first president. Thorpe continued to play professional football until age 41.

Jim Thorpe's medals were returned to his family and his Olympic record reinstated in 1982, almost 30 years after his death.

keepers of the stories or the knowledge of the band or nation. An entire generation lost their culture and their language. Losing native languages meant losing native history as well.

When the Hopi refused to allow their children to be taken to boarding schools, authorities arrested 19 Hopi men for rebelling against government policy, known as "sedition." They spent almost a year in the prison on Alcatraz Island in 1895 and 1896.

Schools were military in nature and required students to wear uncomfortable uniforms. Carlisle was even set up in an old military barracks. School days were often very regimented and included roll call and inspections. At the Cushman Indian School in Tacoma, Washington, the day began at 5:45 A.M. as children rose and made their beds military style. The sound of a bugle playing was often the first and last thing a child heard. A morning and afternoon "free period" was expected to be used at studying, athletics, music lessons, or industrial work.

At Carlisle, half the day was spent on academic work, and the other half was spent on a trade, with more emphasis on trades as children grew older. Boys might learn agriculture or blacksmithing. Girls were limited to the domestic arts, such as cooking, cleaning, and sewing. Children with special talents, such as athletics or art, were allowed to also pursue that. Carlisle was known for its football team where they had a star player and future Olympian in Jim Thorpe.

Other schools used religious study as its only academic work and spent the rest of the day learning trades. In many cases, children were forced to spend their days doing hard labor. Some schools were worse than others, leaving children malnourished and abused. Often, the emphasis wasn't on education but on taking away a child's identity. The BIA oversaw the schools and was supposed to provide supplies. Just as with the Indian agents, the results were uneven: sometimes the supplies arrived; sometimes they didn't.

Obviously, life at the boarding schools was difficult for many children. They were cut off from their families and not allowed to keep anything familiar in their lives. Toys were forbidden except for a brief time at Christmas. For some students, it might be a long time before they could speak to another person, since they had to learn how to use English.

Runaway children were not unusual as extreme homesickness overwhelmed many students. Most runaways were caught and returned to the school. Punishment might come from a strap or being confined to the dorm or even the guard house for a few days.

The schools had their share of sick children. Some died from diseases like smallpox or tuberculosis. A flu epidemic in 1918 was severe at many boarding schools. Over 300 students died at the Haskell School alone. Few children returned to their families in the summer. Many were enrolled in the "Outing Program," in which they lived with white families in town. Some boarding school students were treated as members of the family; others were used as cheap laborers who worked in a home or a farm.

Zitkala-Sa, a Dakota woman who was a graduate of the boarding school system, became a teacher and a writer. She recalled having a difficult time adjusting to school life and often hiding under her bed. One of Zitkala-Sa's published stories was "The Soft-Hearted Sioux." It told the story of a young man who returned to his reservation after being in boarding school. His experience at school left him unable to take part in his former native life.

Many boarding school students who did eventually return home had similar experiences. Bill Wright of the Pattwin tribe was sent to the Stewart Indian School in Nevada at age six. He remembers not being able to communicate with his grandmother and losing his Indian name.

Although some Indian boarding schools lasted well into the middle of the 20th century, most closed down and were replaced by BIA-operated reservation schools. These were later replaced with tribal schools or public schools in the 1970s.

Journaling at Indian School

ZITKALA-SA, A Yankton Sioux, wrote about her first day at White's Manual Institute, a Quaker missionary school for Native Americans.

I cried aloud, shaking my head all the while until I felt the cold blades of the scissors against my neck, and heard them gnaw off one of my thick braids. Then I lost my spirit. Since the day I was taken from my mother I had suffered extreme indignities. People had stared at me. I had been tossed about in the air like a wooden puppet. And now my long hair was shingled like a coward's! In my anguish I moaned for my mother, but no one came to comfort me. Not a soul reasoned quietly with me, as my own mother used to do; for now I was only one of many little animals driven by a herder.

Imagine that you are a student at an Indian school. You must wear unfamiliar clothing and are prohibited from using your native language. What would a day in this life be like? Write a journal entry as if you were this student describing his or her day.

A DAY AT THE CHILOCCO SCHOOL

The Chilocco Indian Agricultural School was one of the U.S. government's earliest Native American boarding schools. Established in 1884 after the Carlisle model, the school originally housed Cheyenne, Arapaho, and Kiowa children, but later students from other Native American nations attended as well.

In the early years, bugles told the children where they needed to be 22 times each day. Itchy, uncomfortable uniforms, limited food, and poor health care were part of everyday life at the school. Students learned agriculture, horseshoeing, printing, shoe repair, tailoring, leatherwork, homemaking, and cooking. Many children remained in the summer to work at the school.

In the early 1900s, Chilocco became an accredited school for up to 12th grade. The elementary school later closed because of low enroll-ment, but the high school remained open. Students learned a school song as well. It started:

Oh Chilocco! Oh Chilocco!
Where the prairies never end,
Oh Chilocco! Oh Chilocco!
You are still our famous friend.
School of schools you are the best,
You're the school that stands the test,
You're the school that brings us fame,
Ever we'll revere thy name.

Schools like Chilocco that continued into the 1930s tended to improve. More emphasis was placed on academic work, and boys and girls could finally sit together in the dining room. Chilocco's doors closed for good in 1980.

The Haskell Institute, 1908.

One Indian school that survives today started as a trade school in 1884 in Lawrence, Kansas. The Haskell Institute evolved over the years to serve the needs of native students. In 1970, Haskell became a junior college focusing on academics. In 1993, the junior college became

Haskell Indian Nations University, and today is known as a center of Native American education and cultural preservation.

Special art programs were developed at the University of Oklahoma and Santa Fe Art School. At the University of Oklahoma, the head of the School of Fine Arts, Oscar Brousse Jacobson, was introduced to Kiowa students from a mission school in Anadarko, Oklahoma. Susie Peters, who worked for the Anadarko Indian agency, had sent some of the drawings to Jacobson, and he was impressed. Jacobson invited six students to study at the university in the late 1920s. Five boys and one girl came to study with Jacobson. James Auchiah, Spencer Asah, Jack Hokeah, Stephen Mopope, Monroe Tsatoke (Hunting Horse), and Lois Smokey were provided with studio space, art supplies, and a living stipend. The young men became known at the "Kiowa Five." They, Lois Smokey, and the other Kiowa art students who came to study at the University of Oklahoma during the next few years shook up the art world and received international attention. Native American art became highly collectible.

Many amazing artists emerged from this period. One of them was Allan Houser (1914–94), a Chiricahua Apache who was born in Oklahoma and studied at New Mexico's Santa Fe Art School. Houser produced work and taught art for many years. As a painter and wood sculptor, Houser was honored in 1954 by the French government for outstanding achievement as a teacher and artist. In the 1960s, Houser started the sculpture department at the Institute of American Indian Art in Santa Fe, New Mexico. He created approximately 1,000 sculptures in stone, wood, and bronze during his lifetime.

Other Native Americans looked for other ways to become contributing members of American society. For some, this meant fighting alongside the very people they had been fighting against for so long.

War Heroes

NATIVE AMERICANS have been fighting in the American military for almost 200 years and have been represented in every military action since the War of 1812, including the Spanish-American War. Many military leaders see the "warrior tradition" as a definite asset during wartime. But perhaps the great wartime contributions came during the two world wars of the 20th century.

Approximately 12,000 native men from many different nations served during World War I. Many Cherokee and Choctaw from the new state of Oklahoma served with the 142nd Infantry of the 36th Texas-Oklahoma National Guard Division.

Modern poster art from the New York City WPA Art Project, created by artist Pistchal between 1936 and 1941.

Decipher a Code

CRYPTOLOGY, THE use of codes, has been used by the military in campaigns around the world for thousands of years. The American military sends messages by code to other Americans. If the coded message is intercepted, it's hoped that the enemy won't be able to decipher it. When Native Americans joined the military during World War I and World War II, some were able to help by sending coded messages in their native languages. In World War I, the army used the Choctaw language to send codes. It's believed that the code helped the Americans win the Mousse-Argonne battle in the final days of World War I. All together, six tribes participating in code talking in World War I.

In World War II, Comanche and Navajo languages were among the 13 native languages used as codes. The greatest number of code talkers, about 420, came from the Navajo tribe. These men have been recognized as warriors and heroes.

The Navajo language, or Diné Bizaad, is a very difficult language to learn if you aren't raised speaking it. At the time of World War II, most Navajo lived on their reservation, so the language was confined to that region. Within the military, the Navajo language was used both as a Type One Code, where a Navajo word stood for an English letter, and as a Type Two Code, which was a translation. Use the excerpt of the *Navajo Code Talker's Dictionary* to decode the Type Two coded message below.

Navajo code talkers. Courtesy of the Navajo Code Talkers Association

Message:
GAH-TAHN AH-HA-TINH. JO-KAYED-GOH NIH-DZID-TEIH SHIL-LOH.

You can find the complete *Navajo Code Talkers' Dictionary* at: www.history.navy.mil/faqs/faq61-4.htm

ANSWER: *Take action. Request runner immediately.*

Navajo Code Talkers' Dictionary

Revised as of 15 June 1945

(Declassified under Department of Defense Directive 5200.9)

Word	Navajo	Literal Translation
abandon	YE-TSAN	run away from
action	AH-HA-TINH	place of action
affirmative	LANH	affirmative
approach	BI-CHI-OL-DAH	approach
baggage	KLAILH (B)	baggage
battle	DA-AH-HI-DZI-TSIO	battle
beach	TAH-BAHN (B)	beach
been	TSES-NAH-NES-CHEE	bee nut
camp	TO-ALTSEH-HOGAN	temporary place
camouflage	DI-NES-IH	hid
casualty	BIH-DIN-NE-DEY	put out of action
cause	BI-NIH-NANI	cause
code	YIL-TAS	peck
deliver	BE-BIH-ZIHDE	deer liver
demolition	AH-DEEL-TAHI	blow up
direct	AH-JI-GO	direct
drive	AH-NOL-KAHL	drive
each	TA-LAHI-NE-ZINI-GO (D)	each
engineer	DAY-DIL-JAH-HE	engineer
extend	NE-TDALE	make wide
fail	CHA-AL-EIND	fail
force	TA-NA-NE-LADI	without care
friendly	NEH-HECHO-DA-NE	friendly
garrison	YAH-A-DA-HAL-YON-IH	take care of

guard	NI-DIH-DA-HI	guard
guide	NAH-E-THLAI	guide
have	JO	have
headquarter	NA-HA-TAH-TA-BA-HOGAN	headquarter
hospital	A-ZEY-AL-IH	place of medicine
immediately	SHIL-LOH (I)	immediately
increase	HO-NALH	increase
intelligence	HO-YA (I)	smart
jungle	WOH-DI-CHIL	jungle
kill	NAZ-TSAID	kill
leave	DAH-DE-YAH	he left
liaison	DA-A-HE-GI-ENEH	know other's action
limit	BA-HAS-AH	limit
machine gun	A-KNAH-AS-DONIH	rapid fire gun
map	KAH-YA-NESH-CHAI	map
medical	A-ZAY	medicine
native	KA-HA-TENI	native
now	KUT	now
number	BEH-BIH-KE-AS-CHINIGH	what's written
objective	BI-NE-YEI	goal
observe	HAL-ZID	observe
occupy	YEEL-TSOD	taken
particular	A-YO-AD-DO-NEH	particular
personnel	DA-NE-LEI	member
primary	ALTSEH-NAN-DAY-HI-GIH	first position

question	AH-JAH	ear
reach	IL-DAY (R)	reach
ready	KUT (R)	ready
request	JO-KAYED-GOH	ask for
runner	NIH-DZID-TEIH	runner
sabotage	A-TKEL-YAH	hindered
scout	HA-A-SID-A-L-SIZI-GIH	short raccoon
smoke	LIT	smoke
supply ship	NALGA-HI-TSIN-NAH-AILH	supply ship
take	GAH-TAHN	take
tank	CHAY-DA-GAHI	tortoise
torpedo	LO-BE-CA	fish shell
under	BI-YAH	under
unidentified	DO-BAY-HOSEN-E	unidentified
vicinity	NA-HOS-AH-GIH	there about
village	CHAH-HO-OH-LHAN-IH	many shelter
vital	TA-EH-YE-SY	vital
warning	BILH-HE-NEH (W)	warning
when	GLOE-EH-NA-AH-WO-HAI	weasel hen
where	GLOE-IH-QUI-AH	weasel here
will	GLOE-IH-DOT-SAHI	sick weasel
yard	A-DEL-TAHL	yard
zone	BIH-NA-HAS-DZOH	zone

THE NAVAJO LONG WALK

Like other native nations, the Navajo were subject to abuses by the U.S. Army. With the help of frontiersman Kit Carson, thousands of Navajo were rounded up for resettlement in 1864. Carson and his men burned every hogan (home) that they could find. As winter approached, many Navajo people, with no homes or food, surrendered. They traveled more than 450 miles by foot from their homeland in western New Mexico to Fort Defiance. Similar to the Trail of Tears, many died on the trail from cold or starvation. This forced journey is known as "The Navajo Long Walk." Two years later, a treaty was signed that allowed the Navajo to return home.

During that conflict, a group of eight Choctaw men in the 36th Division proved invaluable when a commander of one of the companies overheard Choctaw corporal Solomon Lewis and another man, Mitchell Bobb, talking in Choctaw. The commander was frantically trying to figure out a way to get a message to headquarters, but their battalion was surrounded by Germans. The Germans kept breaking U.S. military codes and capturing many of the messengers as well. Could messages sent in the Choctaw language to headquarters work? The company learned that another man fluent in Choctaw, Ben Carterby, was stationed at headquarters and could translate messages back into English.

The eight men were placed in the headquarters of each field company and put to work sending and receiving messages both by radio and through runners. When it appeared to work, 10 more Choctaw men were called into service. Within 72 hours, the tide had turned, and the Americans won some decisive battles to end the war.

Several of these Choctaw soldiers were recognized for their contributions by the French government, but it would take the U.S. government another 90 years to recognize the efforts of the Choctaw code talkers. Unfortunately, none of them lived to see it.

The success of native languages as codes was used again in World War II with several native languages, including Comanche. However, a large number of Germans and Japanese had studied in the United States between the two wars, making it more difficult to use native languages. In fact, all but one language was broken by the enemy. No one could break the Navajo code.

The Navajo language was limited to the Navajo reservation, an isolated piece of land about the size of West Virginia that includes parts of both New Mexico and Arizona. The Navajo language is a complex, unwritten language using syntax and tone that is virtually impossible to learn without extensive exposure to it.

Two hundred Navajo were initially recruited by the Marines, but about 540 men eventually served in the corps during World War II. The Navajo code talkers baffled Japanese code breakers while serving with the U.S. Marines in the Pacific from 1942 to 1945. The Navajo code talkers made it possible for the United States to win the battle at Iwo Jima, a decisive victory. That win resulted in one of the most famous photos of the war, that of six solders raising the U.S. flag atop Mount Suribachi. One of the men was Ira Hayes, a member of the Pima tribe.

Because of the success of the Navajo code, military strategists and leaders kept the code classified until 1968. The Navajo Code Talkers were unrecognized heroes who were asked to keep their actions secret until the military officially recognized them in 1992. Almost 60 years after their military service, President George W. Bush presented the Navajo Code Talkers Congressional Medals of Honor in 2001.

Approximately 44,000 Native Americans fought in World War II, integrated into other units. At home, more than 40,000 Native Americans supported the United States by leaving the reservations to work in wartime industries.

For many Native American men, military service has allowed them to be warriors again. It also allowed Native Americans and nonnative Americans to work together to defend the United States. According to Senator Ben Nighthorse Campbell, a Cheyenne who served in Korea, "There was a camaraderie [in the Air Force] that transcends ethnicity when you serve your country overseas in wartime."

Self-Government Returns

CONDITIONS FOR Native American soldiers in World War II had improved over those during World War I. Perhaps that was because things were slowly changing at home. When the Choctaw code talkers were fighting in World War I, the United States government didn't even recognize them as citizens. Congress eventually granted citizenship to Native Americans in 1924, although it would take more than 30 years before all the states permitted Native Americans to vote in state elections.

Another improvement was the Wheeler-Howard Act, also known as the Indian Reorganization Act. It was passed in 1934 to allow Indian nations to return to self-government and restored tribal ownership of the land. Within specific Native American nations, tribal governments and courts were set up and constitutions written. Efforts to resume cultural traditions began.

Another piece of legislation, the Johnson-O'Malley Act, contracted with states to provide education, health care, and welfare programs on reservations. A 1946 Indian Claims Commission looked at claims where native land was lost due to government misconduct. In its 32 years of operation, more than $1 billion was returned to Native Americans.

CHANGE in INDIAN COUNTRY

IN 1940, most Native Americans lived on reservations, while only 8 percent lived in urban areas. After World War II, urban populations began to rise, particularly for Native Americans. However, this time it wasn't soldiers and guns that convinced Native American bands to move, it was the promise of improved economic status. At the beginning of the 1950s, the average white person earned twice as much as the average African American—$4,000 compared to $2,000 a year. Yet the average Native American on a reservation earned only $950. It was exactly the motivation that the government needed for persuading Native Americans to leave reservations so that the government could close them down.

Moving from the Reservations

LIFE ON reservations during the mid-20th century wasn't easy. Poverty was a way of life for many, often accompanied by rampant unemployment and illiteracy. With such poor living conditions came skyrocketing alcoholism and suicide. These conditions contributed to the lowest life expectancy of any cultural group in the United States. Poisoned groundwater and soil from mining activities near or on reservation land also contributed to low life expectancy. Still, most people weren't motivated to leave the reservations because that was where their communities were.

The federal government officially started the Urban Relocation Program in 1952 with the hopes of eventually terminating reservations. Approximately 200,000 Native Americans took part in this program and moved from reservations to urban areas such as Chicago, Los Angeles, San Francisco, Denver, St. Louis, and Dallas. Others left on their own until more than half the Native American population lived in cities.

The Urban Relocation Program provided one-way bus fare and assistance with housing and employment. BIA relocation officers identified people on the reservation, often young adults, to relocate. Other relocation officers helped "relocatees" adjust to the city when they arrived. People in the Urban Relocation Program were supposed to receive temporary housing, job assistance, and other community resources, plus enough money to get through the first four weeks. For a family of four, this meant $80 a week.

Some people found jobs, but others didn't. Sometimes the change was just too different and people couldn't adjust. While life was economically better for some urban Native Americans, it came at a price. People were cut off from their native roots. Just as children had suffered from a loss of identity when removed to boarding schools, so did many young Native American adults and families who moved from reservations to cities.

People had a better chance of adjusting to city life when they had contact with other Native Americans, even those who belonged to a different nation or band. American Indian Centers provided places where they could go to be with others who understood their culture. Powwows, health care, and cultural traditions all brought people together in the cities. In this way, people adopted Pan-Indianism, when the focus of their identity changed from the specific one of band or nation to the larger one of being Native American. Intertribal marriages

Native Americans often faced discrimination when they left the reservation.

increased, resulting in children claiming membership in two or more Indian nations.

Meanwhile, society was changing. Activism was popular, particularly for young Americans who protested for civil and equal rights and against the Vietnam War. Stirrings of protest were heard in Native American communities as well.

AIM: The American Indian Movement

ONE OF the first native civil rights groups was the National Congress of American Indians (NCAI), founded in 1944 for people with Native American ancestry. BIA employees with an Indian heritage could join but could not be NCAI officers in case there was any bias that came from working for the BIA. The NCAI worked on issues important to people on reservations, including voting rights. The 1968 Indian Civil Rights Act also focused on reservations by requiring states to get tribal consent before acting on issues that would affect a reservation. An outgrowth of the NCAI was the National Indian Youth Council composed of students interested in civil rights issues and nonviolence.

Toward the end of the 1960s, Native American activist groups began forming in urban areas. In 1968, one-third of Native Americans

Native American Numbers

NATIVE AMERICANS are one of the few cultural groups in America that show drops in population. Look at the data on the following table.

Native American Population in the United States, 1850–1990

YEAR	TOTAL
1850	400,764
1860	339,421
1870	313,712
1880	306,543
1890	248,253
1900	237,196
1910	265,683
1920	244,437
1930	332,397
1940	333,969
1950	377,273*
1960	551,669
1970	827,268
1980	1,420,400
1990	1,959,234

* Beginning in 1950, includes Alaskan Natives

Sources: U.S. Census Office, Indians Taxed and Indians Not Taxed in the United States (except Alaska) at the Eleventh Census: 1890 (Washington, D.C.: GPO, 1894), Edna Lee Paisano; Historical Census Statistics on Population Totals by Race, 1790 to 1990, And By Hispanic Origin, 1970 to 1990, for the United States, Regions, Divisions, and States by Campbell Gibson and Kay Jung

Based on what you've learned, explain the differences in numbers. What would account for the 1850 population to be almost cut in half 50 years later? An increase is seen in the 1910 census, but then drops again. Finally, the 1990 census number shows a huge increase when compared to 1950. Why is that?

The map shows the density of the Native American population in the year 2000. What does the map tell you? Research the Native American population of your state for the past 100 years. What kind of trends do you see? Can you explain the changes in numbers?

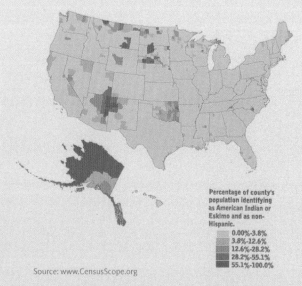

Percentage of county's population identifying as American Indian or Eskimo and as non-Hispanic.

0.00%-3.8%
3.8%-12.6%
12.6%-28.2%
28.2%-55.1%
55.1%-100.0%

Source: www.CensusScope.org

in Minnesota lived in Minneapolis. Members of the Anishinabe nation established a patrol to monitor police harassment in predominately native neighborhoods of the city.

In July of 1968, three of these Anishinabe—Dennis Banks, Clyde Bellecourt, and Mary Jane Wilson—founded the American Indian Movement, better known as AIM. Unlike other civil rights groups, AIM focused on empowering Native American nations through enforcing treaty rights. AIM often looked to tribal elders for guidance for reconnecting to their cultural heritage. "Red Power" was a term associated with some actions and events, such as the 1969 occupation of Alcatraz Island. As the longest occupation of a federal site by Native Americans, the protest on Alcatraz gained media attention, and encouraged many Native Americans to join forces.

Takeover at Alcatraz

NATIVE PEOPLE have a long history with Alcatraz, the rocky island in the San Francisco Bay. Long ago, some tribes used Alcatraz as a place to isolate tribal members who broke a law, but it was also a good place for gathering bird eggs and sea life. During the mission years, some native Californians escaped to Alcatraz in order to keep from being prisoners of the mis-

sion. When California became a state, Americans decided that Alcatraz would make a good location for a prison.

Both military prisoners and civilians were incarcerated on Alcatraz. Among them were many Native Americans. In January 1895, the largest single group of Indian prisoners was sentenced to confinement on Alcatraz when the U.S. government arrested, tried, and imprisoned 19 Moqui Hopi at Alcatraz Island for refusing to allow their children to be taken from their families and sent to Indian boarding schools. Indian people continued to be confined as prisoners in the disciplinary barracks on the island through the remainder of the 1800s and the early 1900s.

In 1964, six Lakota men briefly occupied the island under terms of the 1868 Fort Laramie Treaty. The incident was largely ignored until it was attempted again five years later. One of the first Native American events to capture the attention of the media and the American public at large was this 1969 occupation of Alcatraz.

By 1969, the prison had long been closed and the island abandoned. A group of Native Americans calling themselves the Indians of All Tribes stated that Alcatraz should be converted to a Native American cultural center. Led by Richard Oaks and Adam Fortunate Eagle, the 40-member Bay Area Council of American Indians took possession of the island on November 20, 1969.

They drove claim sticks into the ground to symbolize the discovery sticks used by Lewis and Clark over 150 years earlier. The activists offered to buy Alcatraz from the federal government for "$24 in glass beads and red cloth," the same price paid for Manhattan Island.

The initial group of protestors was soon joined by 90 more, mainly native college students. Usually, the island had approximately 100 people on it at all times. Twenty-two-year-old LaNada Boyer (Means), the first native student admitted to the University of California at Berkeley, stayed the entire 19 months.

The occupation of Alcatraz was one of the first big events for future activists and politicians such as Wilma Mankiller, John Trudell, and Russell Means. Mankiller called Alcatraz the catalyst for her political awareness. Protestors worked on short- and long-term needs, establishing a kitchen, health center, and school. A radio broadcast from Alcatraz by Trudell received a lot of attention. Humor was often used to make a point, such as a plan to start a Bureau of Caucasian Affairs patterned after the BIA. Toy bows and arrows were shot at Coast Guard boats that came too close. Grace Thorpe, daughter of athlete Jim Thorpe, provided supplies such as a generator and brought more attention to the occupation by arranging visits from supportive celebrities such as Marlon Brando and Candice Bergen.

The number of occupants dwindled as students returned to school and individual groups at Alcatraz disagreed with one another about the direction of the protest. Authorities eventually removed the remaining protesters, but several policy changes have been credited to the occupation of Alcatraz, including improved education and health care.

Like the Black Panthers, AIM believed that the only way to deal with the government over present and past grievances was through direct confrontation. While AIM members included the college educated, it also included urban native people struggling to survive. Other cities began starting their own AIM chapters. When AIM reached 75 chapters in 1971, it became a national organization. Its symbol was an upside down American flag, a symbol of distress.

AIM staged events with powerful messages, starting on Thanksgiving in 1970. After painting Plymouth Rock red, Native American protesters took control of the *Mayflower II*, a replica of the original ship, to protest the 350th anniversary of the arrival of the *Mayflower*. Along with other Native American groups, AIM participated in the Trail of Broken Treaties. Just as the 1963 March on Washington promoted civil rights for African Americans, Native Americans hoped that the 1972 Trail of Broken Treaties caravan would do the same for native people. After stopping at important historical sites,

Alcatraz Island. Courtesy of San Francisco Convention and Visitors Bureau

various Native American civil rights groups met in Washington, D.C., to present a 20-point proposal to the federal government. Officials refused to meet with what they viewed as a militant group with unreasonable demands. Some of those 20 requests included:

◆ *Restore the making and following of treaties while investigating treaty violations.*
◆ *Allow Native American leaders to address Congress.*
◆ *Form a Joint Congressional Committee to rebuild Indian relations.*
◆ *Abolish the Bureau of Indian Affairs and create an office of Federal Indian Relations.*
◆ *Protect religious freedom and cultural integrity.*

RUSSELL MEANS

Russell Means, an Oglala Lakota, was born in 1939 on the Pine Ridge Reservation in South Dakota. He was an early leader in AIM, participating in both the Trail of Broken Treaties and the siege at Wounded Knee. During the takeover of the BIA building during the Trail of Broken Treaties, Means gained access to files that revealed the forced sterilization of native women. He brought attention to this very important issue at a later protest, the Longest Walk.

Since his years as an activist with AIM, Means has remained politically active, even running for president on the Libertarian Party ticket in 1988. Since the 1990s, Means has been involved in the entertainment industry, mainly as an actor in such films as *The Last of the Mohicans.*

When BIA officials refused to meet with AIM members, the AIM took over the BIA building. A human barricade kept police from removing AIM members from the building. Protestors left after officials agreed to look at the 20-point proposal. Madonna Gilbert Thunderhawk and Russell Means collected one and a half tons of documents from BIA files that revealed abuses against Native Americans, including the forced sterilization of women. The FBI began monitoring AIM as an extremist group. For ten years, FBI agents kept identified AIM members under surveillance, resulting in 18,000 pages of information. Much of the information about policies and leadership came from a network of sources the FBI had developed.

Native women had important roles in many protests, such as the fish-in protests in Washington during the 1960s and '70s. Historically, people of the Northwest depended upon fishing to feed their families. Although the 1854 Medicine Creek Treaty guaranteed the Northwest native people access and use of natural resources, Native Americans who fished off reservations were being arrested. The fish-ins began in 1964 as nonviolent protests until Washington law officials and vigilantes used clubs, tear gas, beatings, and shootings to drive away the protestors. The protestors, primarily women, began arming themselves for protection.

In 1974 the Supreme Court decided in favor of honoring tribal treaty rights in the *United States v. Washington State*. Also known as the Boldt decision, native communities were allowed half of the annual salmon harvest.

Meanwhile, AIM became the go-to organization for communities where injustices against Native Americans were ignored. In Gordon, Nebraska, the family of Raymond Yellow Thunder wanted his death investigated, but officials refused, saying that he died of exposure. When AIM members arrived, they staged a two-day protest and encouraged people to boycott Gordon businesses until another autopsy was performed. The second autopsy revealed a brain hemorrhage. Yellow Thunder had been beaten to death. After the AIM protests, authorities arrested two Caucasian brothers, Melvin and Leslie Hare, for Yellow Thunder's death. They were convicted and sentenced to a year in prison.

But the biggest event for AIM was still to come.

Wounded Knee Revisited

The Pine Ridge reservation in South Dakota had the distinction of being the poorest place in America in 1973. More and more reservation land was being leased to cattle ranchers, and secret plans were underway to begin uranium drilling. Meanwhile, the unemployment rate at Pine Ridge, home to the Oglala Lakota people, was at 90 percent. It also had one of the highest murder rates—over 100 native people had been murdered in surrounding towns that year.

Much of the trouble was pinned to a corrupt tribal chairman, Dick Wilson, who, among other things, signed over about 200,000 acres of reservation land to the U.S. government. When many traditional Oglala people demanded Wilson's impeachment, his private army of GOONs (Guardians of the Oglala Nation) began assaulting those who opposed Wilson. Oglala women elders asked AIM for help.

The reservation was being described as a place of civil war. According to residents Ellen Moves Camp and Arlette Loud Hawk, U.S. marshals with guns were a common sight, including marshals on top of the BIA building, ready to shoot. Tribal Chairman Wilson had prohibited any type of gathering, even powwows. According to Loud Hawk, "If you wanted to go to Pine Ridge, you had to go in a group to be safe and to ensure that you come back alive. So we knew in order to survive we needed to be in groups. We couldn't be alone. Because if they got somebody alone, they killed them. And there's people that are not found because they killed them and did away with their bodies."

There had been clashes between AIM, supported by many traditionalists, and the current

Fishing for salmon.

BIA-supported tribal government. Wilson had barred AIM from coming onto the reservation, but a group of women elders contacted Dennis Banks and Russell Means, who arrived in February 1973. In the first meeting with AIM in Calico, the women told Banks and Means about the deaths of their children and grandchildren by violence during Wilson's term of office. The women suggested holding another Wounded Knee in remembrance of ancestors who had lost their lives.

Approximately 200 activists took over the Wounded Knee village, calling it the Oglala Sioux Nation. The Oglala people and their supporters held onto Wounded Knee as tribal police, FBI, and federal marshals surrounded them. Many bullets were exchanged. Media attention on the occupation of Wounded Knee was seen around the country, and the majority of the American public supported the Oglala people. Carter Camp, one of the leaders at the Wounded Knee takeover, called Wounded Knee "a powerful symbol to Indian people . . . that changed Indian Country."

Larry Levin, one of several pilots who flew over the reservation to make a food drop reported seeing roadblocks and armored military vehicles surrounding Wounded Knee on day 50. He and his co-pilot, Bill Zimmerman, said it looked like they had flown into a war zone. Along with over 1,500 pounds of food, they sent a message to the protestors. "To the Independent Oglala Nation and their friends at Wounded Knee: Your struggle for freedom and justice is our struggle. Our hearts are with you."

On the 71st day, AIM and the traditionalists agreed to end the occupation if the federal government would began a full investigation into

LEONARD PELTIER

Leonard Peltier (Anishinabe, Dakota, and Lakota) grew up on two North Dakota reservations, the Turtle Mountain Chippewa and Fort Totten Sioux. When Peltier was about 14 years old, the federal government began its Relocation Program, which was designed to terminate reservations. Many people were very angry, and this convinced him that warriors were still needed to protect and defend Native American people.

As an adult, Peltier protested in support of native fishing rights and participated in the takeover of Fort Lawton, an abandoned Washington fort that, by treaty, belonged to native people of the area. After this, Peltier continued his activism by joining AIM. He was a part of the Trail of Broken Treaties march and the takeover of the BIA building in Washington, D.C.

Peltier was accused of the attempted murder of a Milwaukee police officer, a charge that was eventually dropped. While he was in jail, the siege at Wounded Knee occurred. Although Peltier went underground, he still appeared around the country to assist Native Americans in need. This eventually took him back to the Pine Ridge Reservation to see what could be done to help the Oglala people. Peltier was assisting with the running of a sweat lodge ceremony when a shootout with FBI agents led to their deaths. Peltier was arrested and convicted of their murders.

Peltier has consistently maintained his innocence. Over 30 years later, there continue to be FBI documents related to this incident that haven't been released. People from all walks of life, including politicians and actors, have urged officials to release Peltier.

their grievances. The FBI arrested 565 people, mainly AIM members and male Oglala, although 85 women were charged. John Trudell, cochairman of AIM at the time, reported that too much of AIM's energy went into defending the people on trial. As an organization, AIM lost its momentum as it became increasingly fragmented after eight months, the longest federal trial in U.S. history. Meanwhile, violence against the Lakota continued.

Just two years later, FBI agents came onto the Pine Ridge reservation stating that they were looking for an Oglala who had been charged with theft and assault. Shots fired under confusing circumstances resulted in the death of two agents and one AIM member. Another AIM member, Leonard Peltier, was charged and convicted of the murder of the two FBI agents. He remains in prison as of 2010.

Peltier professed his innocence of the crimes. Since his arrest, dozens of petitions and protests have taken place. In 1979, AIM leader John Trudell led a protest at the Supreme Court in Washington, D.C. Hours later, a mysterious fire killed Trudell's wife, three young children, and mother-in-law at their home on the Nevada Duck Valley Reservation. According to Trudell, the FBI did not investigate. He resigned as AIM cochairman.

Although AIM and other civil rights groups faded from the spotlight or disbanded, their

INDIAN HEALTH SERVICES

As part of the Department of Health and Human Services, Indian Health Services provides health care for up to 1.9 million Native Americans and Alaskan Natives of federally recognized tribes or nations. While promises of providing health care to Native Americans have a long history, an organized system didn't come about until the passage of the Indian Health Care Improvement Act in 1976. The law was proposed after studies found that the overall health of Native Americans ranked far lower than that of other groups. Urban and tribal health care programs provide health care to Native Americans regardless of health insurance status. Since the inception of broader health services for Native Americans, life expectancy has increased nine years, although it's still less than the general population.

actions were remembered. President Nixon dropped the plan to terminate the reservations. More attention was focused on the needs of Native Americans, including education and health. In 1972, the Indian Education Act created an Office of Indian Education with funding for bilingual and bicultural programs, including appropriate teaching materials for Native American education. This was followed in 1975 with the passage of the Indian Self-Determination and Education Assistance Act, which increased programs and access to programs that provided education and other necessary services. The act also allowed Indian nations more power within their tribal governments.

Alaskan Natives

DURING THE 20th century, the native people of Alaska began to receive more attention from the rest of United States. Although the origin of the word "Eskimo" is unclear, many think it originated from a Cree word meaning "raw meat eaters" or an Ojibwa word for "snowshoe netter." Regardless, many Inuit people feel that "Eskimo" is a derogatory word. There are three main groups of native people from Alaska: Aleut, Yup'ik, and Inuit. These are broad divisions based on language, and within these larger groups are smaller bands.

Alaskan Natives place a lot of importance upon the extended family. Perhaps the geographical distance from the rest of the United States has allowed the Alaskan Natives to retain more of their traditional beliefs and customs.

At one time, the most important man in a band was the whaling captain. He had to be wealthy to be able to afford boats and equipment. Members of a captain's crew were often his extended family. Today, the equipment is slightly more modern, but whaling continues to be a chief subsistence activity for many native communities. In the autumn months, whalers take to the open sea in motor boats. In

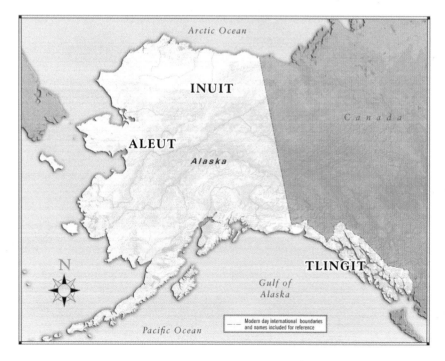

Alaskan drummer, early 1900s.

the spring, whaling crews camp on the edge of the ice.

Regulatory groups and environmental issues have limited the amount of whaling that can be done, yet whaling is also a ceremonial activity for many communities. Ceremonies show respect for the whale. When the wife of the whaling captain pours fresh water into the newly caught whale, it's believed to help the whale's soul return to the spirit world. As with other Native American cultures, every part of the animal is used. Whale meat, skin, and blubber are distributed to everyone in the community. Alaskan Natives have deep ties to the animals and land around them. Environmental concerns like global warming and endangered animals affect their entire culture.

In order to live off nature in extreme weather conditions, Alaskan Natives had to be physically and mentally fit. One way to prepare for the hardships of daily life was to gather in villages for athletic games and contests. Similar to the Olympics, these games tested speed, agility, strength, and endurance. These gatherings were also a time to share news, stories, and friendships.

The tradition of village athletic games was re-created in 1961 with the World Eskimo Olympics. It started as part of the Fairbanks Golden Days Celebration, with performances

Alaskan Native family, early 1900s.

99

What's in a Name?

THE UNITED States is a country of many states, cities, rivers, and lakes. The British and Dutch named many places in the Northeast, often referred to as New England. The Dutch New Amsterdam became the city of New York, named after Britain's Duke of York. The boroughs Brooklyn, Harlem, and Staten Island kept their Dutch-originated names. Spanish names found their way through Florida and the Southwest, from the first American city of St. Augustine, Florida, to California's largest cities of Los Angeles and San Francisco. The French added New Orleans, St. Louis, and Des Moines.

Although Europeans took many things away from Native Americans, including Native American languages, many place names that originated from Native American languages are still used today.

Use an atlas, encyclopedia, or the Internet to match the following place names with the originating tribe and translation.

1. Mississippi

2. Oklahoma

3. Seattle

4. Lake Ontario

5. Missouri

6. Yosemite

7. Tallahassee

8. Nebraska

9. Arizona

10. Massachusetts

A. (state) "place of the small spring," Tohono O'odham tribe

B. (state & river) "people with dugout canoes," Missouria

C. (state & bay) "at the range of hills," Massachuset

D. (state) "flat or broad water," Sioux/Lakota/Dakota

E. (national park) "those who kill," Central Miwok

F. (state capitol) "tribal land," Seminole

G. (city) name of Native American, Duwamish/Suquamish

H. (state) "red people," Choctaw

I. (state & river) "large river," Algonquian

J. (lake) "beautiful lake," Iroquois

ANSWER: 1-I, 2-H, 3-G, 4-J, 5-B, 6-E, 7-F, 8-D, 9-A, and 10-C

---

by Alaskan Native dance groups. Athletes competed in the blanket toss, high-kick, and seal skinning during the three-day event. Each year the crowds and competition increased.

In the early 1970s, two decisions were made. First, women's competitions were established. And second, the name was changed to the World Eskimo-Indian Olympics. The event adopted a symbol of six interwoven rings to represent the major Alaskan Native groups: Aleut, Athabascan, Inupiaq, Yup'ik, Haida, Tlingit, and Tsimpsian.

Freedom of Religion

THE YEAR 1978 was an important one in returning religious rights to Native American families. Native Americans have a long history of not being allowed to follow traditional religions and customs, beginning with the early Spanish who forced Christianity on different nations. While Christianity continues to be important in Native American communities, some people also practice native religions. One of these, the Native American Church, has been a focus of attention for its use of a hallucinogenic plant called peyote.

The 1978 Religious Freedom Act stated that Native Americans, Alaskan Natives, and Native Hawaiians have the right to practice traditional religions. This law also protects sacred sites used for worship. However, the law's interpretation is regularly challenged in courts. For example, during the 1980s, a logging company wanted to construct a logging road through the sacred land of the Yurok, Karok, and Tolowa nations of California. The courts sided with the logging company and U.S. Park Service to allow the building of the road.

In another situation, Alfred Smith and Galen Black were fired from their jobs at a drug rehabilitation organization because of peyote use during a ceremony within the Native American Church. Their unemployment benefits were also denied. The two men argued that these decisions violated their rights to freedom of religion, and the Oregon Court of Appeals and Oregon State Supreme Court agreed. But when Oregon took the case to the U.S. Supreme Court, the decision was reversed, with the court stating that the State of Oregon was allowed to deny unemployment benefits because peyote use violated Oregon drug laws.

Because of the particular circumstances of Native American religion, lawmakers passed the American Indian Religious Freedom Act Amendments of 1994. One of the things it did was allow peyote to be used in a religious ceremony.

Native Americans have a long history of spirituality, but there are many different spiritual beliefs and practices among Native Americans. Many Native American churches combine native traditions with Christian religion. For example, hymns may be sung in both English and native languages. A "cedaring" may follow a preacher giving a sermon. Cedaring is a ceremony or ritual used with the smoke of cedar. It is used to cleanse, purify, or bless people or buildings.

INDIAN CHILD WELFARE ACT

Native American children have been taken from their parents for hundreds of years. From the late 19th century until the middle of the 20th century, children were removed for placement in Indian Boarding Schools. Still another issue has been the removal and placement of native children in foster care or adoptive white families at much higher rates than other cultural groups. Often, officials removed native children based upon cultural differences, ignoring the importance of the extended family in a Native American child's life.

In 1978, Congress passed the Indian Child Welfare Act for the purpose of keeping the care of native children within their tribes. The custody of native children is transferred to tribal courts when possible, which recognizes that placement with extended family or within the tribe is preferable to outside placement when a child's parents can't take care of him or her.

TRIBAL RIGHTS
and CULTURAL PRIDE

TODAY'S NATIVE Americans live throughout the United States with a variety of occupations and lifestyles. Many Native Americans today face special challenges in their identity. Do they identify first with a specific native tribe or nation, or to a broader identification as a Native American, American Indian, or First American? Many of today's Native Americans also claim nonnative heritages as well, and the question remains as to how much white culture should be part of their lives.

Native Americans face significant problems with stereotypes from the population at large. Schools often have Native American curriculum units that teach the past of the indigenous people of America. However, this history is often generalized for large groups of people. Just because members of a specific Native American nation rode horses or wore feathers in their hair or paint on their faces doesn't mean all Native American nations did. Nor does it mean that any of today's Native Americans do this any more than a white American wears a coonskin cap or lives in a log cabin.

Pretending to be Native American when you're not is very disrespectful, particularly with false and stereotypical language or dress. So is calling a Native American "chief" unless he or she really holds that title within a specific nation. The United States has a long history of disrespect toward its first inhabitants and their descendants. It's time to treat everyone with respect.

Legislation

LEGALLY, "INDIANS" means indigenous people of the United States from the time of colonization, including Alaskan Natives and Native Hawaiians. The federal government recognizes some of the groups—bands, tribes, or nations—as "domestic, dependent nations." Federal recognition means a government-to-government relationship allowing specific Native Americans to receive government services, from education to health care to protection of resources. Some Native American communities have been recognized by the state they live in but have been unsuccessful at gaining federal recognition, which is a long and expensive process.

Federal and state legislation continues to try to balance past and present wrongs. One of the past wrongs was the removal of human remains and objects by anthropologists and archaeologists. The 1990 Native American Grave Protection and Repatriation Act made it illegal to buy or remove human remains. Furthermore, the law states that human remains and sacred objects that have been removed without tribal consent must be returned to the rightful people.

The extinction of some native languages and the risk of losing even more of Indian culture led to the Native American Languages Act, also passed in 1990. This law supports the preservation and use of native languages within individual Native American nations and in schools.

Native people who make a living through arts or crafts have their work protected by the Indian Arts and Crafts Act. This law requires that any work promoted as Native American work must be the work of an artist who is a member of a federally or state-recognized tribe.

Today's Issues

As with all populations, there are issues affecting Native Americans that must be addressed. For many nations, tribal sovereignty remains the most important. Legal issues constantly arise when recognizing native nations as independent nations within U.S. borders. Native American nations must determine what constitutes membership within a nation as well. This issue affects economic development. Since laws have been passed that allow gaming on Native American land, some nations have become economically successful through the profits from casinos.

With more than half of all Native Americans living in urban areas, some feel cut off from their tribal identity and extended families. Native American cultural centers and powwows help people stay connected to their heritage.

While health care has improved, Native Americans as a whole have higher rates of alcoholism, substance abuse, diabetes, and tuberculosis. More needs to be done. Suicide is the second leading cause of death, after accidents, among Native American youth. Overall, three times as many native youth (from 15 to 24 years of age) commit suicide than the same age group in the overall population. Some areas, such as Lakota reservations, have an even higher rate of suicide.

With daily news on the hazards of pollution and global warming, the environment is an important native topic as well. Historically, Native Americans have had a close relationship to the Earth. Many reservations are located on land where erosion has made it unusable. Big dam projects contributed to land problems. While oil and minerals discovered on Native American land have brought additional funds to some tribes, removing the minerals has destroyed large portions of land in addition to poisoning the water and contributing to health problems.

The Black Mesa coal-slurry pipeline, running from northern Arizona to Laughlin, Nevada, takes over a billion gallons of water from the Hopi and Navajo each year. Cyanide mining pollutes water on the Fort Belknap Reservation in Montana. The Western Shoshone and Mdewakanton Sioux are fighting against nuclear testing and a nuclear power plant bordering their reservations in Nevada and Minnesota. Some bands with significant poverty have agreed to accept hazardous waste sites on tribal land for increased funding.

Science, Art, and Politics

Today's Native Americans are teachers, scientists, artists, musicians, writers, politicians, doctors, nurses, and more. Native American pride has increased as more Native Americans become known for their contributions in music, films, and books. Native American musicians play everything from traditional flute music to heavy metal. You can listen to rock music by Stevie Salas, hip-hop from Dago Braves, gospel from Janelle Turtle, new age by Carroll Medicine Crow, country music from Tracy Bone, blues from Jimmy Wolf or Jim Boyd, or metal from Rage Against the Machine.

Here are just a few of today's other well-known Native Americans:

Enoch Haney:
Artist, Politician, Principal Chief

Born in Oklahoma, Enoch Kelly Haney is a member of the Seminole nation. His family arrived before statehood, and many of the Haney men served as leaders of the Seminole nation.

Haney recalls being pulled toward art at a very young age, whether creating original works of art at the age of two or later digging clay from the riverbank for a bust of Abraham Lincoln. He continued his artistic education at Bacone College, the University of Arizona, and Oklahoma City University. Although he started his professional art career as a painter,

he became an accomplished sculptor whose work has earned many honors and is known throughout the world. In anonymous judging, Haney's sculpture *The Guardian* was chosen to sit on top of the Oklahoma State Capitol in 2003. This 17-foot-high sculpture of a Native American male with a lance firmly in the ground weighs slightly over four tons. Haney turned down the $50,000 commission fee, saying that the statue was a gift to the State of Oklahoma.

As the first full-blood Native American in the Oklahoma Legislature, Haney served as a state representative from 1980 to 1986 and a state senator from 1986 to 2002. During his tenure in the state legislature, Haney served as the chairman of the Appropriations Committee, developed and implemented alternative education programs, and participated in the executive committee of the National Conference of State Legislators.

After more than 20 years in state government, Haney returned to service in the Seminole nation, where he had been active in tribal politics before his election to the state government. In 2005, Haney was elected Principal Chief of the Seminole Nation of Oklahoma.

Other recent well-known Native American leaders include Wilma Mankiller (Cherokee), Ben Nighthorse Campbell (Northern Cheyenne), and Carol Juneau (Hidatsa/Mandan).

Maria Tallchief, Dancer

BORN ON an Oklahoma reservation in 1925, Osage tribal member Maria Tallchief began music and dance lessons at a young age, and it soon became evident that she was meant for ballet. She is considered one of the foremost American ballerinas. In her 20s, she met and married famed choreographer George Balanchine, who was inspired to create great ballets for her. Tallchief danced in many famous roles, including *The Nutcracker* and *Swan Lake*. She belonged to some of the most important dance groups, including the American Ballet Theatre. After retiring from dancing in 1965, Tallchief became the artistic director for the Chicago Lyric Opera Ballet and later founded the Chicago City Ballet.

Other Native Americans in the arts include filmmaker Chris Eyre (Cheyenne/Arapaho), painter R. C. Gorman (Navajo), and composer Steven Alvarez (Mescalero Apache).

John Herrington, Astronaut

JOHN HERRINGTON, a member of the Chickasaw nation, became the first Native American in space aboard the space shuttle *Endeavour* in 2002. To recognize his cultural heritage, Herrington took a flute, an eagle feature, and a Chickasaw nation flag into orbit.

Born in Wetumka, Oklahoma, Herrington earned a bachelor's degree in applied mathematics and a master's degree in aeronautical engineering. He was a navy aviator for many years before being selected as an astronaut in 1996. Herrington completed a two-year astronaut training program at Johnson Space Center in Houston, Texas, in 1998. His 2002 mission included a space walk. As a pilot, he has logged over 3,800 flight hours on dozens of various aircraft.

Since 2005, Herrington has worked as a commercial test pilot and been active with Rocketrek (www.rocketrek.com), a program that encourages students in science, technology, engineering, and mathematics.

Other Native American scientists include chemist Dr. Jani Ingram (Navajo), plant ecologist Dr. Robin Kimmerer (Potawatomi), and biologist Dr. David Burgess (Cherokee).

Sherman Alexie, Author

ONE OF the most important writers in adult and children's literature today is Sherman Alexie of Seattle. Alexie's writings about modern Native Americans make readers laugh and cry, sometimes at the same time!

Alexie (Spokane/Coeur d'Alene) grew up on the Spokane Reservation. He had to undergo brain surgery at six months of age. When he survived, doctors predicted that he would suffer severe mental retardation. The doctors were obviously wrong about Alexie, who read *The Grapes of*

John Herrington became the first Native American in space in 2002. Courtesy of http://spaceflight.nasa.gov

Wrath at age five, but he did suffer from seizures throughout his childhood. As a teenager, Alexie chose to go to high school off the reservation in hopes that he would get a better education. The only Native American at his school, he excelled academically and in basketball.

Alexie attended college with plans of being a doctor, but when he repeatedly fainted in his human anatomy class and also discovered poetry in his English class, he changed his mind. Alexie excelled at writing and received two poetry fellowships. One year after college, he had two collections of poetry published. He followed this with a short story collection, *The Lone Ranger and Tonto Fistfight in Heaven*. After more publishing, Alexie wrote a screenplay for the movie *Smoke Signals*, which won two awards at the Sundance Film Festival. Known for his great sense of humor, Alexie sometimes performs standup comedy.

His first book for young adults, *The Absolutely True Diary of a Part-Time Indian*, has won many major awards, including the National Book Award, the ABBYA Top 10 Book for Teens, the 2009 Odyssey Award, and the 2008 Boston Globe–Horn Book Awards for Excellence in Children's Literature in Fiction.

Other Native American writers include Steven Judd (Kiowa/Choctaw), Paula Gunn Allen (Pueblo/Lakota), and Pulitzer Prize winner N. Scott Momaday (Kiowa).

Wes Studi, Actor

BORN IN Nofire Hollow, Oklahoma, Wes Studi is a respected actor and director who has been involved with countless films and television specials. A member of the Cherokee nation, Studi attended the Chilocco Indian School (see page 82) where he learned the English language. A Vietnam veteran, Studi's first film appearance was in the cult classic *Pow Wow Highway*, although he spent years working in television before that. He has made more than 50 appearances on the big and small screens, including such popular films as *Dances with Wolves*, *The Last of the Mohicans*, *Heat*, and *Thief of Time*. Studi is also a musician and sculptor.

Other Native American actors include Graham Greene (Oneida), Floyd Red Crow Westerman (Santee Dakota), Litefoot (Cherokee), Tantoo Cardinal (Cree), Adam Beach (Ojibwa), and Irene Bedard (Inupiat Eskimo/Cree).

Notah Begay, Athlete

NATIVE AMERICAN athletes have been breaking records since Jim Thorpe's days. When Navajo golfer Notah Begay shot a 59 on the PGA tour at the age of 24, he became only the third person to do so. In 1999, he became the first Native American to win a PGA tour. Begay says that his success as an athlete comes from his Navajo heritage.

Other Native American athletes include Olympic gold medal runner Billy Mills (Lakota),

A Family Tree

LEARNING ABOUT your family history and origins can be a rewarding experience. Once you have information you can start creating a family tree, a visual representation of your family. Find out more about your history in this activity.

1. Research Your Family Name.

Using information from your family and the Internet, see if you can track down the origin of your family name (surname). What nationality does it come from? Does your surname have a special meaning?

2. Learn from Older Family Members.

No doubt you hear family stories whenever relatives come together for reunions or holidays. Ask if there are family letters or Bibles that might have information. However, your biggest resource will be older family members, such as your grandparents. Start with yourself and work backward. Record names, birthdates, marriages, and dates of deaths. Where did these family members live? Where were they born? What were their occupations?

3. Create a Family Tree.

With a large piece of paper, draw a small vertical line at the bottom center of the paper to represent the trunk of your "tree." Write your name directly above the trunk. Make horizontal lines next to your name to represent your siblings.

Draw two parallel lines coming up from your name. Put each of your parents at the top of a line. Next to their names, you can write their siblings—your aunts and uncles.

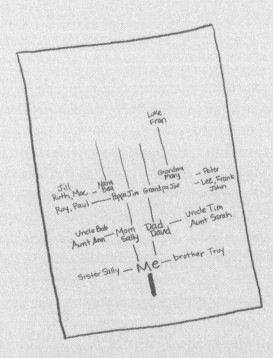

Above your father's name, you will fill in his parents, and so forth. Do the same for your mother's "branch" of the family. Get complete names, particularly maiden names of women. The further you go back, the more last names will be added to your family tree. Add birthdates and birthplaces if you can.

How far can you go back? Chances are that you will find some gaps. You can do research to fill in some of the gaps. Databases, Social Security records, birth and death registries, and old newspapers can sometimes provide more answers. Genealogy libraries located in many communities can help people with their research.

Imagine not being able to go back for more than a few generations because the history of your family has been destroyed. How does that make you feel?

Celebrate Your Heritage

Powwows are a celebration of being Native American. There was a time when the government prohibited Native American tribal ceremonies and dances, so holding these celebrations is a source of pride for many today. Plan a celebration of your own heritage. Think of special clothing, activities, and sharing that you can do with others that will honor your heritage.

Courtesy of Indian Health Services

Boston Red Sox outfielder Jacoby Ellsbury (Navajo), and hockey player Judd Blackwater (Blackfoot).

Native American Genealogy

WE OFTEN hear relatives say things like, "You look just like Aunt Rose," or "You act just like your grandmother's cousin." Perhaps you share a name with a great-great relative that you never met. It might make you curious about this person or other people in your family who came before you.

Genealogy—tracing your ancestors or family tree—is a popular hobby because people like to know where they came from. If you're Native American, it can be hard to find information about your family history. For one thing, Native Americans often depended upon oral history, but when children were sent to boarding schools and forced to forget the language of their parents and grandparents, those stories were lost. Likewise, when children were adopted into other families, stories about family history weren't passed down.

If you have, or suspect that you have, a Native American heritage, gather as much information as you can from talking to older relatives and looking at their old photographs and papers and anything else that will lead you to full names and tribal affiliations. Once you have a full name and affiliation, some tribal offices can help you locate more information. Some Native American genealogy sites that may be helpful include:

Dawes/Freedman Roll Search—NARA Archival Information Locator: www.archives.gov/research/arc/native-americans-final-rolls.html

"Dawes Rolls" at Access Genealogy: www.accessgenealogy.com/native/finalroll.php

Native American Genealogy: www.native-languages.org/genealogy.htm

Cultural Pride

PRIDE IN Native American heritage is catching. Many Native American tribal government offices have seen an increase in people tracing their native roots. Another way Native Americans celebrate their heritage is through powwows. A powwow is a Native American celebration of people coming together to share traditions, food, song, and dance. Originally a custom of the Plains tribes, powwows are now held throughout North America—in auditoriums or on county fairgrounds. People may come from far away to attend a powwow lasting several days.

Many annual celebrations take place, from Labor Day festivities and fairs to remembrance activities for the Trail of Tears. Pan-Indian celebrations such as the Red Earth Cultural Festival and the Gathering of Nations draw large crowds from all over North America. The Gathering of Nations is an annual event held each April on the University of New Mexico campus in Albuquerque. Started in 1983, the Gathering of Nations promotes the culture and traditions of Native American communities. Activities include powwows, a marketplace, and a Miss Indian World contest. Some tribal powwows are limited to tribal members or by invitation only. Many other powwows are intertribal, meaning they are open to all tribes and nonnative people as well.

A circle is the center of the powwow. Singers and drummers sit in the middle of the circle while people dance clockwise around them. Dancers of all ages, from very young children to the elders, enjoy going to the circle. The drum in the center of the circle is sometimes compared to the heartbeat. Every powwow begins with its "heartbeat" before singers begin singing about war, honor, and family. Songs are shared in a native language or as "vocables," syllables and chants easily taught to people of other tribes.

The "Grand Entry" signals the beginning of the dancing. Dancers enter the arena, following the Head Man Dancer and the Head Lady Dancer, people chosen by the host of the powwow for their abilities and personal qualities. Every dance has a purpose or name. Some dances are limited to certain families, tribes, or a type of dance. "Fancy dancing" is when men, and occasionally women, dance dressed in colorful tribal regalia that may include headdresses. Intricate tribal designs of ribbons, feathers, and beads swing as a dancer twirls and stomps at a frenzied pace, feet or even knees touching the ground quickly. The jingling of bells or an occasional war cry is occasionally overheard. Even as a spectator, the sight of fancy dancing takes your breath away.

Other types of dancing include "grass dancers" whose clothing is decorated with streaming yarn. Women dancers may participate in the "jingle dress dance" with cloth dresses decorated with tin cones that make a tinkling sound when they move. Sometimes dancers compete against each other in dance competitions.

Everyone is invited to dance during intertribal dancing. Participants dressed in street clothes or traditional buckskin or colorful cloth outfits take steady steps clockwise around the circle. Feet quickly adapt to the beat of the drum. Women carry shawls either over their shoulders or folded over their arms and held in front.

Powwows often include "give-aways" as part of the celebration. The host of the event or the families of the Head Dancers give gifts to honored people.

Exhibit Your Life

PEOPLE LEARN a lot about Native Americans, particularly Native Americans of the past, through museum exhibits. Pretend that you want people 1,000 years in the future to know something about your life. Design a museum exhibit to show a person from the future what your life was like.

Try to use a variety of media. Remember that electronic media are dependent upon an energy source, and photographs usually fade over time. What else could be in your exhibit?

The National Museum of the American Indian

THE HISTORY and culture of Native Americans have been a significant part of many natural history and art museums for some time. But in 1989 President George H. W. Bush signed a law to establish the National Museum of the American Indian (NMAI) as a part of the Smithsonian Institute. Although smaller facilities opened in both Maryland and New York City, the principal museum opened on the National Mall in Washington, D.C., on September 21, 2004, between the National Air and Space Museum and the U.S. Capitol building.

As the first national museum dedicated to Native Americans, NMAI brings Native American leaders, musicians, poets, dancers, artists, and scholars to educate the millions of visitors. According to director, Kevin Gover (Pawnee/Comanche), people from all over the world have been educated and enlightened at NMAI.

GLOSSARY

alliances agreements to work together

allotments equal shares or parts

ancestral related to people of the past whom a person is descended from

anthropologist a person who studies the ways of life of people of different cultures

archaeologist a person who learns about the past by digging up and examining objects

archaic old and not used anymore

artifacts objects of the past made by humans

assimilation the process of absorbing something into another body, group, or culture

bias preferring one person or point of view more than another

bilingual being able to speak two languages well

clan a large group of families

confederacy a union of states, tribes, or people with common beliefs and goals

culture the life, customs, and traditions of a group of people

descendants children, children of your children, and so forth

directive instructions issued by someone in authority

epidemic an infectious disease that spreads through the population

ethnologist a person who studies human races and characteristics

exposure harmful effect of severe weather on a person

extinct when something such as an animal or plant has died out

genocide extermination of a race of people

heritage important traditions handed down from generation to generation

homesteader a settler on a piece of land

immigration the process of coming to another country to live permanently

indigenous native to a specific area; can be people, animals, or plants

infectious able to be spread from one person to another through germs or viruses

intolerant unwilling to accept someone else's thoughts or behavior

irrigation the supply of water to crops by artificial means

kerosene a colorless fuel made from petroleum

kiva a chamber, at least partially underground, used for ceremonies or meetings in Pueblo villages

liaison communication or cooperation between two people or groups

linguist a person who studies languages

mammoth an extinct animal that looked like a large, shaggy elephant

mesa a hill with steep sides and a flat top

migration the process of moving from one country or region to another

mission a church or other place where missionaries live and work

missionaries people sent by a religious group to teach that group's faith to others

nation a large group of people who share the same language, customs, and government; a nation of people usually live in the same region

origin the point where something began

paleontologist a person who studies fossils and ancient life forms

peninsula a piece of land surrounded by water on three sides, but attached to a larger land mass

petroglyph a drawing or carving on rock made by ancient people

policy a general plan or framework that helps people make decisions

proclamation a public announcement

provisions a supply of food or other basic items

ranchero ranch or rancher

reservation an area of land set aside by the government for a specific purpose

resource something valuable or useful

sacred holy; something deserving great respect

sacrificial the offering of something to a god

sovereign independent; also a king or queen

strategist a person who creates a plan to achieve a military victory or a goal of some kind

syntax grammar rules that dictate how words should be put together to make sentences

treaty a formal agreement between two nations

tribal of or belonging to a tribe

tribe a group of people who share ancestors and a culture

warfare the fighting of wars

RESOURCES

Web Sites to Explore

We Shall Remain

www.pbs.org/wgbh/amex/weshallremain

THIS WEB site is based on an award-winning PBS series, *We Shall Remain*. The five episodes that originally aired in early 2009 provided historical information from the time of the *Mayflower* until the last siege at Wounded Knee. History was both recited and acted by many of today's most well-known Native American actors. A teacher's guide is also found at the site.

National American Indian Heritage Month

www.nps.gov/history/nr/feature/indian

THIS NATIONAL Park Service site promotes awareness of National American Indian Heritage Month in November by providing information about National Park sites tied to Native Americans. The National Park Service provides historical information and features about individual sites.

Native American History and Culture

www.teacheroz.com/Native_Americans.htm

THIS HISTORY site created by a Texas history teacher provides links to information about Native American history and culture. Included are primary documents, general sites, Native American legislation, and information organized by individual Native American nations.

Carlisle Indian School

www.CarlisleIndianSchool.org

THIS SITE was created by historians Barbara Landis and Genevieve Bell in an attempt to keep the history of the Carlisle Indian School and its students alive. A history of the school is provided, along with primary and secondary resources links. A blog is included.

Sequoyah Research Center

http://anpa.ualr.edu/default.htm

THIS UNIVERSITY of Arkansas Web site is the home of the American Native Press Archives and continues to collect copies of Native American publications, including newspapers and periodicals. The collection covers history, literature, and Native American communities. An important section is the "Trail of Tears" project.

Native American Facts for Kids

www.native-languages.org/kids.htm

THIS WEB site was developed by a nonprofit organization promoting Native American languages. The kids' page offers resources on various historical facts of Native American communities. In addition to languages, information can be found on homes, clothing, food, hairstyles, and more.

Native American History

www.lib.washington.edu/subject/history/tm/
native.html

THIS SITE provided by the University of Washington gives information about general history and tribal and regional histories. It includes a large amount of historical information on Pacific Northwest history too.

That National Archives: Teaching with Documents

www.archives.gov/education/lessons/
fed-indian-policy

THIS FEDERAL government Web site provides information on governmental Indian policy from 1870 to 1900. It concentrates on the period immediately postremoval of the Five Nations from the Southeast to Indian Territory. The Dawes Act and its effects are covered as well.

Mesa Verde National Park

https://imrcms.nps.gov/meve/index.htm

THIS NATIONAL Park Service site concentrates on one of the most well-preserved and extensive examples of cliff dwellings by an Ancestral Puebloan culture. The Web site covers the discovery, individual cliff dwellings, and the artifacts that provide scientists with information about this ancient culture.

National Museum of the American Indian

http://americanindian.si.edu

THE NATIONAL Museum of the American Indian is a part of the Smithsonian Institute. The main museum resides in Washington, D.C., but there is also a center in New York City as well as traveling exhibits. "Native Words, Native Warriors" is an online resource about the Code Talkers of World War II.

The Official Website of the Navajo Code Talkers

www.navajocodetalkers.org

THE NAVAJO Code Talkers Association is an advocacy group that represents the Navajo Code Talkers. The group's Web site provides information and oral histories. The organization is currently working on creating the Navajo Code Talkers Museum and Veterans' Center Project.

Census Scope

www.censusscope.org/us/map_nhindian.html

THE SOCIAL Science Data Analysis Network (SSDAN) provides demographic information about the Native American population and specific tribes/nations based on 2000 census data.

Native Web

www.nativeweb.org

THIS WEB site provides current information about indigenous people all over the world. The Resource Center link provides information about music, literature, events, environment, genealogy, and other resources.

Books to Read

Alexie, Sherman. *The Absolutely True Diary of a Part-Time Indian.* New York: Little Brown and Co., 2009.

Bowen, DuWayne Leslie. *A Few More Stories: Contemporary Seneca Indian Tales of the Supernatural.* Lanham, MD: AltaMira Press, 2000.

Broker, Ignatia. *Night Flying Woman.* St. Paul, MN: Minnesota Historical Society Press, 1983.

Bruchac, Joseph. *The Arrow over the Door.* New York: Dial, 1998.

_____. *Children of the Longhouse.* New York: Puffin Books, 1996.

_____. *Geronimo.* New York: Scholastic, Inc., 2006.

Carvell, Marlene. *Sweetgrass Basket.* New York: Dutton Juvenile, 2005.

Eastman, Charles A. *Indian Boyhood.* New York: McClure, Phillips & Co., (1902) 1971.

Grace, Catherine O'Neill and Marge Bruchac. *1621: A New Look at Thanksgiving.* Des Moines, IA: National Geographic Society, 2001.

Harper, Maddie. *"Mush-hole": Memories of a Residential School.* Toronto: Sister Vision Press, 1993.

Hubbard, Jim, editor. *Shooting Back from the Reservation*. New York: The New Press, 1994.

Johnson, Troy R. *Red Power: The Native American Civil Rights Movement* (Landmark Events in Native American History). New York: Chelsea House, 2007.

Lawson, Michael L. *Little Bighorn: Winning the Battle, Losing the War* (Landmark Events in Native American History). New York: Chelsea House, 2007.

Marra, Ben, editor. *Powwow: Images along the Red Road*. New York: Harry N. Abrams, Inc., 1996.

Medicine Crow, Joseph with Herman J. Viola. *Counting Coup: Becoming a Crow Chief on the Reservation and Beyond*. New York: Random House, Inc., 2006.

Olsen, Sylvia, with Rita Morris and Ann Sam. *No Time to Say Goodbye: Children's Stories of Kuper Island Residential School*. Winlaw, British Columbia: Sononis Press, 2001.

Reynolds, Fiona. *Living through History: Core Book—Native Americans: the Indigenous Peoples of North America*. Portsmouth, New Hampshire: Heinemann Educational Publishers, 2000.

Reynolds, Fiona. *Living through History: Foundation Book—Native Americans: the Indigenous Peoples of North America*. Portsmouth, New Hampshire: Heinemann Educational Publishers, 2000.

Roessel, Monty. *Kinaaldá: A Navajo Girl Grows Up*. Minneapolis: Lerner Books, 1993.

Smith, Cynthia Leitich. *Rain Is Not My Indian Name*. New York: Harper Collins, 2001.

Spooner, Michael. *Last Child*. New York: MacMillan Publishing Company, 2005.

Standing Bear, Luther. *Land of the Spotted Eagle*. Lincoln, Nebraska: University of Nebraska Press, (1933) 1978.

Tingle, Tim. *Spirits Dark and Light: Supernatural Tales from the Five Civilized Tribes*. Atlanta: August House, Inc., 2006.

Waldman, Carl and Molly Braun. *Timelines of Native American History*. New York: MacMillan Publishing Company, 1994.

Wolfe, Alexander. *Earth Elder Stories*. Calgary: Fifth House, 1988.

Wolfson, Evelyn. *Native Americans* (History Explorers series). Kent, England: Ticktock Media, Ltd., 2009.

Zitkala-Sa/Gertrude Bonnin. *American Indian Stories*. Washington: Hayworth Publishing House, (1921) 2003.

INDEX

Italicized page numbers indicate illustrations.
Page numbers with *m* indicate maps.